THE BOOK OF ROCK QUOTES

PUBLISHED IN 1977 BY OMNIBUS PRESS

EXCLUSIVE DISTRIBUTORS:
BOOK SALES LIMITED
78 NEWMAN STREET, LONDON W1P 3LA ENGLAND
BOOK SALES PTY, LIMITED
27 CLARENDON STREET, ARTARMON, SYDNEY
NSW 2064, AUSTRALIA

© COPYRIGHT 1977 BY JONATHON GREEN

COVER DESIGN BY PEARCE MARCHBANK
BOOK DESIGN BY PERRY NEVILLE
ART DIRECTION BY PEARCE MARCHBANK
COVER PHOTOGRAPH BY ROGER PERRY
PHOTO RESEARCH BY SUSAN READY

THIS © COPYRIGHT 1977 BY
OMNIBUS PRESS
ISBN 0.86001.413.4, OP 4026 G

THE BOOK OF
ROCK
QUOTES

Compiled by Jonathon Green.

Omnibus Press
London/New York/Sydney

CONTENTS

FOR WHAT IT'S WORTH
SECTION 1/PAGE 7

AS TIME GOES BY
SECTION 2/PAGE 12

PUPPET MASTERS
SECTION 3/PAGE 17

AIN' THAT A FACT
SECTION 4/PAGE 23

PAYING THOSE DUES
SECTION 5/PAGE 31

SOUNDS & FURIES
SECTION 6/PAGE 35

WORDS OF WISDOM
SECTION 7/PAGE 40

STRUTTIN' YOUR STUFF
SECTION 8/PAGE 45

GOD ONLY KNOWS
SECTION 9/PAGE 49

PAIN IN MY HEART
SECTION 10/PAGE 53

THE WILD AND THE WOOLY
SECTION 11/PAGE 62

WE SHALL OVERCOME
SECTION 12/PAGE 65

SEX WITH STARS
SECTION 13/PAGE 71

THE LOOK OF LOVE
SECTION 14/PAGE 77

GENIUS IS PAIN
SECTION 15/PAGE 81

GROWN UP ALL RIGHT
SECTION 16/PAGE 87

BLOWING IN THE MIND
SECTION 17/PAGE 93

FOR A FEW DOLLARS MORE
SECTION 18/PAGE 97

YOU, THE PEOPLE
SECTION 19/PAGE 101

WHITE LINE FEVER
SECTION 20/PAGE 105

BLACKS & BLUES
SECTION 21/PAGE 109

MIRROR MIRROR
SECTION 22/PAGE 116

IT'S ONLY ROCK 'N' ROLL
SECTION 23/PAGE 121

FOR WHAT IT'S WORTH

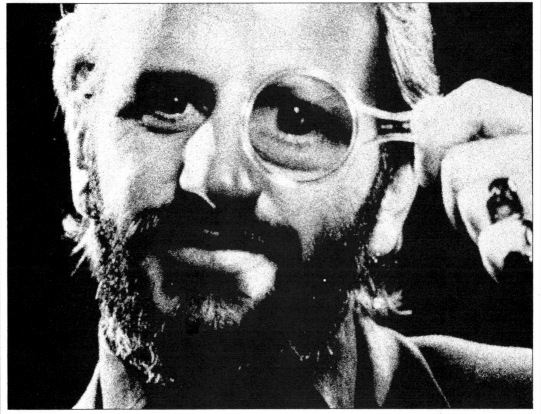

RINGO STARR

America should be proud that John wants to live here.
Ringo Starr

There are forty people in the world and five of them are hamburgers.
Captain Beefheart

When you're dealing with yourself, you're alone.
P. J. Proby (James Marcus Smith)

Ordinary people are the most interesting.
Ray Davies

Middle class kids make the best rock 'n' roll.
Elliott Murphy

Rhythm and blues? It's nothing but rock 'n' roll without the movements.
Mickey Ashman

The people of America are just not born with culture.
Phil Spector

And you think you're so clever and classless and free, but you're still fucking peasants as far as I can see.
John Lennon

A thorough survey may prove that it is impossible to buy a plain white or decently tasteful shirt in the whole of Las Vegas
Jann Wenner, editor 'Rolling Stone' magazine

PAUL SIMON

You can run lots of rules but you know you can't outrun the history train.
Paul Simon

I built more sandcastles in one lifetime than there are pyramids in Egypt.
Arlo Guthrie

You can only live one dream at a time.
Diana Ross

I think the human race will survive only if it's supposed to. I sometimes speculate that it will evolve, temporarily at least, into machines.
Roger McGuinn

Rock music is a necessary step in the evolution of man. As was LSD, Hitler, the electric light and everything else.
Mel Lyman

What is perfect? Perfect is death. It's a physical death. Termination.
Jimi Hendrix

I'd rather be unemployed than dead.
Swamp Dogg

Let's face it, you can't worship a guy for destroying an instrument in the name of rock.
Pete Townshend

Remember that the city is a funny place. Something like a circus or a sewer.
Lou Reed

It's alright letting yourself go, as long as you can let yourself back.
Mick Jagger

We are always searching. I think that now we're on the point of finding.
John Coltrane

All lies and jest still a man hears what he wants to hear and disregards the rest.
Paul Simon

In the end you become part of everything you hate, basically.
Ray Davies

If you got it today you don't want it tomorrow, man . . . 'cos you don't need it . . . cos, as a matter of fact, tomorrow never happens, it's all the same fuckin' day . . .
Janis Joplin

I like sound-effect records. Sometimes late at night I get a mint julep and just sit there and listen to sound effects. I'm surprised more of them aren't on the charts.
Bob Dylan

I believe in what George Harrison says — that you can change the world with love.
Frank Zappa

I learned a lot of good music while I was in the joint.
Judee Sill

I think you have to have laws to live by. If you're plowing a mule out there, I don't think you can jump ahead of the mule. You gotta stay behind the dad-gummed plow.
Jerry Lee Lewis

We're not politicians, we're not painters, we're musical people just like circus people or carnival people and all you can do as musical people is to try to get to the top.
Robert Johnson, producer of Bob Dylan, etc.

The only thing that stands up is whether you've got it or not. The only thing that counts is if you're still around. And I'm still around.
Van Morrison

Colleges are like old age homes, except for the fact that more people die in colleges.
Bob Dylan

A lot of kings throw their crowns around — what's so sacred about a crown?
Bob Dylan

Why the greatest invention in life is the safety pin. The second greatest is perfumed toilet paper.
Tiny Tim

You can't always get what you want but if you try sometimes, you might find, you get what you need.
Mick Jagger and Keith Richard

Oh, I believe in yesterday.
John Lennon and Paul McCartney

If politics deal with prophecy, then good. If it deal with sommat else, then it no good. Now is a wicked time but wickedness come to a perpetual end. Prophecy a fulfil.
Bob Marley

Nothing can really be better than waking up in the morning and everything is still the same as it was the day before. That's the best thing you can have in life, consistency of some kind.
Pete Townshend.

PETE TOWNSHEND/PHOTO BY BYRON NEWMAN

FOR WHAT IT'S WORTH

I think Shakespeare is shit. Absolute shit! He may have been a genius for his time, but I just can't relate to that stuff. 'Thee' and 'thou' — the guy sounds like a faggot. Captain America is classic because he's more entertaining. If you counted the number of people who read Shakespeare, you'd be very disappointed.
Gene Simmons, Kiss

When my envelope arrived marked On Her Majesty's Service, I thought I was being called up.
John Lennon on receiving the MBE

Message songs, as everybody knows, are a drag. It's only college newspaper editors and single girls under fourteen that could possibly have time for them.
Bob Dylan

The colleges have to be destroyed, they're dangerous. Doctors trying to cure the freaks while they gulp pills. Rushing with the music. It's the music that kept us all intact . . . kept us from going crazy. You should have two radios — in case one gets broken.
Lou Reed

LOU REED

Give Peace a Chance.
John Lennon

Better compare us with President Carter, because people vote the same way as they buy records.
Ace Frehley, Kiss

Many a bum show has been saved by the flag.
George M. Cohan

The trouble with superheroes is what to do between phone booths.
Ken Kesey

If we don't survive, we don't do anything else.
John Sinclair

Anyway you choose you're bound to lose in New York City
Paul Simon

We are as Gods and might as well get good at it.
Whole Earth Catalogue

I do believe in equality, but I also believe in distance.
Bob Dylan

Decay turns me off. I'll die first before I decay.
Bob Dylan

Like a good American Robert Johnson lived for the moment and died for the past.
Greil Marcus in 'Mystery Train'

He not busy being born is busy dying.
Bob Dylan

You can't be a feminist and live in a mansion.
Bonnie Raitt

So what if I live with straights. I have straight babies.
Paul McCartney

Ultimately you need someone who's your good friend.
Paul Simon

Jack o' diamonds is a hard card t' play.
Bob Dylan

I don't expect to be singing 'Twist and Shout' when I'm thirty.
John Lennon

Convicts are the best audiences I ever played for.
Johnny Cash

Art, if there is such a thing, is in the bathrooms, everybody knows that. To go to an art gallery . . . that's just a status affair.
Bob Dylan

She knows there's no success like failure, and that failure's no success at all.
Bob Dylan

True cheapness is exemplified by the visible nylon strings attached to the jaw of the giant spider.
Frank Zappa

Progress is Chanel No. 5 on the rocks.
Captain Beefheart (Don Van Vliet)

My life is the street where I walk.
Bob Dylan

Ain't no better place than the US. This is a free enterprise system. You can get whatever you want in the US.
Howlin' Wolf (Chester Burnett)

There are a lot of things you have to sacrifice. It all depends on how deep you want to get into whatever your gig is.
Jimi Hendrix

I can't demand sacrifices at this stage of the game.
Keith Richard

Too many people are obsessed with pop music. The position of rock 'n' roll in our subculture has become far too important. Especially in the delving for philosophical content.
Mick Jagger

I don't think you could any more train a person to be a country music singer than you could train someone to have almond eyes.
Merle Travis

Falling down gets you accepted.
Mick Farren

One thing you can't hide is when you're crippled inside.
John Lennon

I think politics is a valid concept, but what we have today is not really politics. It's the equivalent of the High School election. It's a popularity contest. It's got nothing to do with politics. What it is is mass merchandising.
Frank Zappa

MIKE LOVE

If Kissinger can't impose peace on the earth, we must find an alternative
Mike Love, Beach Boys

The closest Western civilisation has come to unity since the Congress of Vienna in 1815 was the week that the 'Sgt. Pepper' album was released.
Langdon Winner

I am he, as you are he, as you are me and we are all together.
John Lennon and Paul McCartney

You know, I get very emotional when I see other people's record collections. Their choice always get to me. It reflects that person.
Ray Davies

I saw music as a bourgeois jerk-off.
Steve Hillage

I do most of the interviews because the rest of the band are lazy buggers, but our musical policy is definitely democratic.
Phil Lynott, Thin Lizzy

In the future everyone will be famous for fifteen minutes.
Andy Warhol

AS TIME GOES BY

We like this kind of music. Jazz is strictly for the stay-at-homes.
Buddy Holly

The sicker you kids get, the greater the shows we'll have for you.
Alice Cooper

In the old days you'd drag your old man out on the lawn and kick the shit out of each other and he'd say 'Be home by midnight' and you'd be home by midnight. Today parents daren't tell you what time to get in. They're frightened you won't come back.
Frank Zappa

What became of the regulars? Not a helluva lot. None of them became showbiz stars . . . the kids just grew up. Some are gay, some are straight. Some of them are doing very well, some are not.
Dick Clark on the development of the 'American Bandstand' kids after the TV show ended.

It's not music, it's a disease.
Mitch Miller on Rhythm and Blues

We were terribly British, which we all are really under the whole thing. It was hard for us to latch onto this new thing of dressing up like they did and lying on your back playing a bass upside down.
Marty Wilde, in a BBC interview

What a drag it is getting old.
Mick Jagger and Keith Richard

I'm bugged at my old man and he doesn't even know where it's at.
Brian Wilson

The great things about Nazism is that your parents hate it.
Tony James, Generation X

Old man take a look at my life, I'm a lot like you.
Neil Young

I'll take today's teenagers any day to the ruckus rousers and souvenir scalpers who made our lives miserable during the heyday of Goodman and Sinatra. The worst thing these kids do is feed sugar to the horses.
New York City cop, 1959

The sight of an amplifier in a Trad club was a bit like that of the Pope in certain parts of Belfast.
Tom McGuiness

I always thought the good thing about the guitar was that they didn't teach it in school.
Jimmy Page

I don't have a love-affair with a guitar — I don't polish it after every performance. I play the fucking thing.
Pete Townshend, 1965

If I feel like killing a hippie, I will. I don't have to be angry to do that . . . I'm more of a robot than a person.
Sid Vicious, Sex Pistols

Hippies? Why, I'm the original.
Jerry Lee Lewis

Burt Weedon — I thought he was a tailor or something.
Mick Jones, The Clash

How does it feel to be one of the beautiful people?
John Lennon and Paul McCartney

Most Hell's Angels I know are into partying.
Jerry Garcia

ROD STEWART

My moment of stardom was at the Aldermaston marches.
Rod Stewart

They may be world famous, but four shrieking monkeys are not going to use a privileged family name without permission.
Frau Eva von Zeppelin

The weekend begins here!
'Ready Steady Go!' TV show slogan

A lot of people start to fall to bits at thirty — that's why it's dangerous. I don't fall to bits at all. Quite honestly, once you are able to reproduce you're over the hill. You start to go downhill at eighteen, physically.
Mick Jagger

Will you still need me, will you still feed me, when I'm sixty-four?
John Lennon and Paul McCartney

Because they're driven by strange new desires they don't understand! Because they're eager to live all life's fun at once!
Ad for 'Because They're Young' starring Dick Clark and Duane Eddy

MICK JONES

I ain't never lived under five floors up.
Mick Jones, The Clash

I hope we're a nice old couple living on the coast of Ireland or something like that — looking at our scrapbook of madness.
John Lennon

She (we never thought of ourselves) is leaving (never a thought for ourselves) home (we struggled hard all our lives to get by).
John Lennon and Paul McCartney

I smash guitars because I like them. I usually smash a guitar when it's at its best.
Pete Townshend, 1965

We're another generation. They're rich and living in another world altogether . . . to them it's just another way of making money. They're not playing for the kids. They're not playing for us. To them it's just another nine to five job.
Joey Ramone on Sixties Rock Establishment

I hope this verdict will be a lesson to the young people of this country — that you just can't go into a person's house and butcher them up.
Marie Mesmer, one of Manson trial jury

These boys (the Beatles) have genius. They may be the ruin of us all.
Bert Berns, writer of 'Twist and Shout', 'Hang On Sloopy' etc.

I know there's some people terrified of the bomb, but there are other people terrified to be seen carrying a modern screen magazine.
Bob Dylan

If Hitler were alive today, the German girls wouldn't let him bomb London if the Beatles were there.
Anonymous

We know a lot of people don't like us because they say we're scruffy and don't wash. So what! They don't have to come and look at us do they? If they don't like me, they can keep away.
Mick Jagger, 1964

The singer'll have to go, the BBC won't like him.
Eric Easton, on being shown the Rolling Stones by Andrew Loog Oldham

We like to look sixteen and bored shitless.
David Johanssen, New York Dolls

If your children ever found out how lame you are, they'd kill you in your sleep.
Frank Zappa

I have built a clean, bright set and I want it filled with clean, bright people who enjoy jazz.
Johnny Stewart, producer of BBC-TV's 'Trad Fad' and later of 'Top of the Pops'

People try to put us down just because we get around. Things they do look awful c-c-cold. Hope I die before I get old.
Pete Townshend

Come mothers and fathers throughout the land, and don't criticize what you don't understand.
Bob Dylan

When I put on that guitar, I'm Eric Clapton and Elvis Presley. It's the fountain of youth.
Al Kooper

One week he's in polka-dots, the next week he's in stripes 'cos he's a dedicated follower of fashion.
Ray Davies

All of my friends at school grew up and settled down, then they mortgaged up their lives . . . they just got married 'cos there's nothing else to do.
Mick Jagger and Keith Richard

Boy, this punk rock thing . . . it's so phoney. They're not for-real tough guys.
Wayne Kramer, MC5, in a letter to Mick Farren

It was not a happy childhood. I mean, when your father blows his head open, it's not funny.
Phil Spector

I'm a time traveller. To me it's still 1970. I've been moving backwards at the speed of light. I think the punk rock thing is rubbish.
Ian Anderson, Jethro Tull

You walk out of the Amphitheater after watching the Rolling Stones perform and suddenly the Chicago stockyards smell clean and good by comparison.
Tom Fitzpatrick, 'Chicago Sun Times'

You've got to pick up every stitch. Beatniks are out to make it rich.
Donovan Leitch

I tell you man, Wisconsin is the ultimate territory. I'm convinced we're a mid-West group.
Frank Zappa

The old are scared of us. They don't want the change. It makes them irrelevant to what's going on now and they know it.
Johnny Rotten, Sex Pistols

I don't know if you think much of me but someday you'll understand. Wait till you learn how to talk, baby, I'll show you how smart I am.
Randy Newman

RANDY NEWMAN

JIMI HENDRIX & NOEL REDDING

They say we are obscene and vulgar . . . but I don't let them hang us up . . . we just get excited by the music and carried away.
Jimi Hendrix

America has known many rebellions — but never one like this. Millions of teenage rebels heading for nowhere. Some in 'hot rod' cars, others on the blare of rock 'n' roll music, some with guns in their hands, and at their head — a dead leader.
'Picture Post' on the death of James Dean, 1956

JAMES DEAN

Counting the cars on the New Jersey Turnpike. They've all come to look for America.
Paul Simon

Don't you give me no dirty looks. Your father's hip, he knows what cooks. Just tell your hoodlum friend outside you ain't got time to take a ride.
Leiber and Stoller

Come and see us Poppa, when you can. There'll always be a place for my old man. Just drop by when it's convenient to. Be sure and call us before you do.
Randy Newman

Something is happening here but you don't know what it is, do you, Mr. Jones?
Bob Dylan

Your mother she's an heiress, owns a block in St. John's Wood. And your father'd be there with her, if he only could.
Mick Jagger and Keith Richard

I was born with a plastic spoon in my mouth.
Pete Townshend

When our kids are grown, with kids of their own, they'll send us away to a little home in Florida. We'll play checkers all day until we pass away.
Randy Newman

You're too old and your hair's too long.
Johnny Rotten, Sex Pistols

Goodbye all you punks. Stay young and stay high. Hand me my cheque-book and I'll crawl off and die.
Pete Townshend

We still have the code of the street.
Mick Jones, The Clash

I have a whole army wardrobe. We're prisoners of peace. It's like some people were captured by the Viet Cong, I feel I've been captured by society, born in captivity. TV made everything easy.
Steven Soles, Alpha Band

Lots of people who complained about us receiving the MBE received theirs for heroism in the war — for killing people. We received ours for entertaining other people. I'd say we deserve ours more, wouldn't you.
John Lennon

PUPPET MASTERS

I want to manage those four boys. It wouldn't take me more than two half days a week.
Brian Epstein, November 9th, 1961

I was the Elvis of South Africa
Mickie Most

Mickie Most is just terrible. He treated Lulu horribly.
Maurice Gibb

If you can survive in this line of work, then you can survive in the jungle. I know I'm a mixed character, but it's horses for

courses. If someone's being rough with you, you gotta be rough back.
Peter Grant, manager of Led Zeppelin

I'd rather the Mafia than Decca.
Keith Richard

The trouble is that so much of the record business is being run by people who don't have a clue what it's about.
Paul McCartney

Darling, we're broke. David has been robbed blind. There were millions but other people got them, not us. It's the usual story with pop musicians. David has taken people to court but in the end he found it too unbearable to get involved at that sort of game — it simply puts you on their level.
Angie Bowie, in the 'Evening Standard', 1977

Why shouldn't I get 20 per cent? I cured all their problems.
Allen Klein

I was certain that 'Fabe' was it and it was going to happen. But if it hadn't, I simply would have looked for someone else and built him.
Bob Marucci, owner of Chancellor Records, teen stars

Some of this music is so intellectual that it is a little like the poet T. S. Eliot with his seven layers of ambiguity in each line.
Mort Nasatir, head of MGM Records, on Ultimate Spinach, front-runners of the 'Boston Sound'.

When I first knew Elvis he had a million dollars worth of talent. Now he has a million dollars.
Colonel Tom Parker

DAVID & ANGIE BOWIE

People say I made the Rolling Stones. I didn't. They were there already. They only wanted exploiting.
Andrew Loog Oldham

I want to make it clear that Elektra is not the tool of anyone'a revolution. We feel that the revolution will be won by poetics, not politics — that poetics will change the structure of the world.
Jac Holzman, President of Elektra Records

Who gives a damn if a camera comes into shot?
Jack Good, pioneer of TV Rock Shows

Well I'm sitting here thinking just how sharp I am, I'm the necessary talent behind every rock 'n' roll band.
Mick Jagger and Keith Richard

You've got to have a few villains in this business, or nothing would get done.
Richard Cole, road manager for Led Zeppelin

You can always come back, but you've got to come back better. If you come back worse, or even the same, you're dead.
Phil Spector

At Apple we are only interested in ideas that will make us a million dollars a day.
Peter Brown

This could turn out to be what we call a 'black matzoh' in the trade. That means when you can't sell them you have to eat them.
Richard Mason, head of Telemark Records, on the failure of 'Hang In There, Mr. President' to help Richard Nixon.

We just hope we keep running into people who think they know where we're going, so they'll take us there and we won't have to worry about it.
Howard Kaylan, Flo and Eddie

The game of artist-manager is a very tricky game . . . the manager doesn't have a union. He is a manager only because he and the talent say he is. He doesn't have any other qualification. It's a bastard art.
Jon Hartmann, sometime go-fer for Colonel Tom Parker

I'd rather try and close a deal with the Devil.
Hal Wallis, producer of nine Presley pictures, on Colonel Tom Parker

It wasn't so much that Brian Epstein discovered the Beatles but that The Beatles discovered Brian Epstein.
Paul McCartney

These boys won't make it. Four-groups are out. Go back to Liverpool, Mr. Epstein, you have a good business there.
Verdict of Beatles' first record audition in London.

I never signed a contract with the Beatles. I had given my word about what I intended to do and that was enough. I abided by the terms and no-one ever worried about me not signing it.
Brian Epstein

While money doesn't talk, it swears. Obscenity, who really cares, propaganda, all is phoney.
Bob Dylan

All promoters think about is an ass in every seat.
Jonny Podell, big-league booker

I suppose there are two things I miss: I often think it would have been nice to have had a mother when I was a little boy, and yes, sometimes I think it would be quite nice to be considered a good guy.
Allen Klein

You get to the point where you have to change everything — change your looks, change your money, change your sex, change your women because of the business.
Mick Jagger

It's what's in the grooves that counts.
Corporate slogan, Tamla Motown Records

Only a pawn in their game.
Bob Dylan

Hell hath no fury like a hustler with a literary agent.
Frank Sinatra

We were just following orders. And we liked following orders. It was easy because we didn't do anything, we just did what we were told. We had a hit single, people screamed, and we thought if we could follow these orders exactly that was about as good as you could possibly do.
Rick Derringer on his career with The McCoys

I'd like to live up to my reputation of being a nice guy.
Colonel Tom Parker

Joe Walsh is an Eagle now, and as such doesn't speak to the Press.
Irving Azoff, manager, The Eagles

There is only one Establishment — *Rolling Stone* and the *New York Times* are the same.
Terry Knight, former manager, Grank Funk Railroad

I knew Roy Orbison's voice was pure gold, but I felt he'd be dead inside a month if people saw him.
Sam Phillips, Sun Records

Writing little symphonies for the kids.
Phil Spector

Bow Tie Daddy.
Frank Zappa

The trouble is, you're a fucking idealist and I'm a whore.
Dick Clark, once 'Czar of the Switchblade Set', M.C. of TV's 'American Bandstand'

In an industry riddled with drug addicts, homosexuals and hangers on, I am one of the few real men left.
Ron Arden, sometime manager Small Faces, Amen Corner, The Move, ELO, etc.

The Beatles are now my secret weapon.
Sir Alec Douglas-Home, Prime Minister 1964

I shall consider it my patriotic duty to keep Elvis in the 90 per cent tax bracket.
Colonel Tom Parker

No two publishers have ever agreed on the exact location of Tin Pan Alley, except that it was usually in close proximity to the source of the next dollar.
Tony Palmer in 'All You Need Is Love'

Limp, you bugger, limp!
Jack Good's exhortation to Gene Vincent on BBC-TV's '6.5 Special'

Make sure you stay ordinary.
Lee Eastman, advising his son-in-law Paul McCartney

I'm like the man who manufactures aspirin. I don't empathize with all those headaches, I just want to sell aspirin.
Kim Fowley, producer

I kept at them, beating their eardrums, because I knew that fame and fortune might distort them.
Murray Wilson, father of Carl, Brian and Dennis Wilson

I gave the Beatles their first tour — I took them to Hamburg before they ever made a record. I gave Mick Jagger his first tour in this country. James Brown was with me. I put Joe Tex in business.
Little Richard

I wouldn't get any satisfaction out of creating a Mary Hopkin.
Mick Jagger, commenting on the Beatles' launch of 'Apple'.

Each tune has a degree of stimulation programmed against the workers' fatigue curve. If you were listening to music at seventy beats a minute it would do nothing for you because that's your pulse rate. It would neither soothe nor stimulate you. In fact we never go below seventy beats because we are not interested in soothing people or putting them to sleep.
Lee Valvoda, executive of the Muzak Corporation

It's like a soup that's out there for three weeks and these maggots come out.
Bill Graham, promoter, on CBS-TV Rock Music Awards 1977

The Man Can't Bust Our Music
Columbia Records slogan, late 1960s

SIR ALEC DOUGLAS-HOME

ARLO GUTHRIE

I don't know, but I've been told that the streets of heaven have all been sold.
Arlo Guthrie

You know what will happen at Wembley? George will announce that he's gonna do a concert, right? About two weeks later Ringo will say 'Hey, I'll play too'. Then John says he's gonna be there, Everyone will wanna know where Paul is. He'll think I'm trying to embarrass him. You betcha! I'll roast his fuckin' ass!
Allen Klein, 1970

Let's have all you people, let's make the sign of peace, people . . . if you could see yourselves . . .
Rikki Farr, organiser of the Isle of Wight Festival, 1970

If it wasn't for the poor man Mister Rich Man, what could you do?
Bessie Smith

I apologise, motherfucker, that I'm a human being. I fucking apologise. Emotional, you're fucking right. Fuck you, you stupid prick! Do you know what emotions are? Stand up and have emotions. Get up and work. Get up and sing. Get up and act. You think I'm an actor. You're full of shit. Man, I have more fucking balls than you'll ever see. You want to challenge me in any way about emotions. You slimy little man. Fuck you. Fuck you! Don't get peaceful with me. Don't touch me!
Bill Graham, promoter, in his resignation speech, 1969

Sell your soul to the company who are waiting there to sell plastic ware and in a week or two, if you make the charts, the girls will tear you apart . . .
Roger McGuinn and Chris Hillman

Whoever is doing the Bay City Rollers' publicity has no sense of shame.
John Peel, BBC Radio One DJ

At least with The Who things haven't been boring.
Chris Stamp, co-manager, The Who

I drove the Beach Boys through the wall. When they were exhausted, I drove them harder, because they asked for it.
Murray Wilson, father of Brian, Carl and Dennis Wilson

The idea that Peter Jenner steered us away from 'Road-runner' and into the realms of psychedelia is crap. And we've got a great battery of solicitors to prove it.
Roger Waters, Pink Floyd

If Tammy Wynette walked up right now and we were recording tonight and I said 'Your next record is "Three Blind Mice" she'd say two words, "What key?"'
Billy Sherill

You guys wanted to be bigger than the Beatles, and I wanted you to be bigger than Mao.
John Sinclair, manager, MC5

If I could find a white man who had the Negro sounds and the Negro feel, I could make a billion dollars.
Sam Phillips, Sun Records

My dream was to invent the word 'producer'.
Phil Spector

Basically it's a sound business decision, because, let's face it — the groups that are associated with hard drugs . . . are very undependable, they're difficult to work with, and they're hard on your sales and marketing people.
Mike Curb, then President MGM Records, on his decision to fire eighteen bands supposedly using drug-orientated lyrics.

We cannot just put together great shows, because then you go bankrupt.
Bill Graham, promoter

The amusing thing about this is its supreme unimportance. After it's all over, and they've outsold everyone else in history, the Monkees will still leave absolutely no mark on American music.
'Crawdaddy Magazine'

The last official get-together I had with the Monkees was when they gave me a six-dollar watch upon my retirement from the group. They all chipped in and even had it engraved. It read 'To Peter, from all the guys at work'.
Peter Tork

You can't get the Monkees back together as a rock 'n' roll group. That would be like Raymond Burr opening up a law practice.
Mike Nesmith

My job is to get that emotion into a record. We deal with the young generation, with people lacking identification, the disassociated, the kids who feel they don't belong, who are in the 'in-between' period in their lives.
Phil Spector

I don't suppose agents will mind me saying that they think people are more or less like cattle.
Ray Davies

Elvis Still King: Col. Still Col.
Headline in 'Rolling Stone' Magazine, July, 1972

Island Records have got gold records on the wall like other people have china ducks.
Richard Thompson

With all due respect, I don't want to manage Ravi Shankar. I'm a businessman. I told Gary 'Don't spiritualise yourself out of the business'. If hymns were hits, I'd be managing Moses.
Dee Anthony, manager of Gary Wright, disciple of Paramahansa Yogananda.

I noticed how industry people are afraid to be tender or gentle.
John Klemmer

The key to building a superstar is to keep their mouth shut. To reveal an artist to the people can be to destroy him. It isn't to anyone's advantage to see the truth. In the long run the audience matters more. That's the story.
Bob Ezrin, producer

Hey, there were some pretty funny things in this script. I'm gonna have to read it some day.
Elvis Presley, after finishing an MGM picture, 1960s

AIN' THAT A FACT

CHUCK BERRY

The only Maybelline I knew was the name of a cow.
Chuck Berry

I don't know anything about music — in my line you don't have to.
Elvis Presley

All my records are comedy records.
Bob Dylan

I'm not a superstar. I started life as a chubby kid and things never got much better.
David Crosby

Responsibility, security, success mean absolutely nothing . . . I would not want to be bach, mozart, tolstoy, joe hill, gertrude stein or james dean. they are all dead. the Great books've been written. the Great sayings have all been said.
from The Sleeve Notes to 'Bringing It All Back Home' by Bob Dylan

All I've done in the world I owe to military discipline.
P. J. Proby (James Marcus Smith)

I'm equal parts Brando and Balenciaga.
Patti Smith

If I was still with Nick and the Red Streaks back in Liverpool, they would never allow me to try to act or design furniture or write things.
Ringo Starr

I know what I am inside. I'm an honest to God story teller and I use my guitar to help me along my way.
Brownie McGhee

Twenty years ago they'd have said I was weird.
Todd Rundgren

We're just a bunch of crummy musicians really.
George Harrison, radio interview, 1962

I couldn't go pop with a mouthful of firecrackers.
Waylon Jennings

In a word, I'm boring.
Randy Newman

We're Pat Boone, only a little cleaner.
Richard Carpenter

I was always a freak. Never a hippie, but always a freak.
Frank Zappa

I'm weird, I really don't play a lot. Most people think that I probably go home to some guitar shop in the sky and practise all day.
Jeff Beck

JEFF BECK

I'm not nervous, I'm just quick.
Johnny Cash

I don't like to be called Elvis the Pelvis . . . I mean, it's one of the most childish expressions I ever heard coming from an adult. But, uh, if they want to call me that, I mean there's nothing I can do about it.
Elvis Presley

I didn't really want to become a hit pop writer . . . I would have loved to have been the guy who thought up the Guinness Book of Records.
Tim Rice

What we do is derivative, very derivative.
Mick Jagger

I want to tell the world how the guy in the filling station feels.
John D. Loudermilk

I was just a hired guitar player when we started.
Keith Richard

I was always the seven stone weakling.
Eric Clapton

Every time folks start to fix up my talkin', it messes with my singin'.
Loretta Lynn

I was always better at naming groups and designing albums.
John Entwhistle

There was a big rumour at Newport in 1965 that I cried when I was booed. I didn't know enough to.
Bob Dylan

We always knew something would happen sooner or later. We always had this blind Bethlehem star ahead of us. Fame is what everyone wants, in some form or another.
Paul McCartney

We didn't set out to look like deranged bank clerks.
Lee Brilleaux, Dr. Feelgood

I'm not a crooner — I'm just a song salesman.
Frankie Vaughan, 1959

My scalp is so sensitive . . . I go crazy when anybody grabs my hair.
David Cassidy

ELTON JOHN

'You know, people think I'm all cuddly and lovely and beautifully pop-starrish. I'm not, really I'm not.
Elton John

Sometimes I wish I could occasionally do a show that wasn't swamped with noise just so I could let some of the older people and the squares hear my songs without interference.
Cliff Richard, 1959

I have this tremendous talent, but it was like putting Einstein's brain into a canteloupe. They didn't give me all the pieces.
Kim Fowley

We all have bad habits. Personally I'm not to good at getting up in the morning and I happen to enjoy scrambled egg for breakfast.
Pat Boone, 1959

For the past ten years all I've had to do is stand in the background, sometimes put on a bit of makeup, and look happy to be there.
Bill Wyman

The trouble with me is that I have to be kicked up the ass, but there's no-one who can do it.
Mick Jagger

Nobody is this business is very stable, else we wouldn't all be up on stages making asses of ourselves.
Kris Kristofferson

There are any number of ways to get from one place to another on the neck of the guitar that I don't know about.
Tom Verlaine, Television

Most of my ideas come from the newspapers.
Gilbert O'Sullivan

'My Generation' was our biggest seller and we never hope or want to produce anything like it again.
Pete Townshend

I hang my laundry on the line when I write.
Joni Mitchell

If I hadn't been a songwriter I'd have liked to have written children's fairy stories.
Roy Wood

Before I got into rock 'n' roll, I was going to be a dentist.
Gregg Allman

I go to bed alright; I wake up twisted.
Ray Davies

When you see me with a smile on my face, then you know I'm a mental case.
Alice Cooper and Michael Bruce

I tried to commit suicide one day. It was a very Woody Allen type suicide. I turned on the gas and left all the windows open.
Elton John

What would I have become if I hadn't joined the Stones? A layabout, but a very high-class one.
Keith Richard

We always make our mistakes in public.
Paul McCartney

The image we have would be hard for Mickey Mouse to maintain.
Karen Carpenter

I would have sold my soul, my ethics, my *anything* . . . to look like other girls.
Mary Travers on having long, straight hair in the 1950s

I'm proud of the group and name, but I think the clean American thing hurt us.
Brian Wilson

I really wanted to become a soccer star. Being up there is the nearest I'll ever come to that.
Rod Stewart

I would like to do something worthwhile, like maybe plant a tree on the ocean, but I'm just a guitar player.
Bob Dylan

You have to be a bastard to make it, and that's a fact. And the Beatles are the biggest bastards on earth.
John Lennon

I don't like rock 'n' roll anyway.
Mick Jagger

Getting myself up in the morning, or should I say afternoon, is like picking at a scab.
Janis Joplin

If they scream at me, it's probably in horror.
Elton John

I have constipated periods which are very depressing.
Kevin Ayers

I don't really know what I am, or where I'm from. I just know I'm not from here.
Marc Bolan

MARC BOLAN/PHOTO BY BARRY PLUMMER

AIN' THAT A FACT

'Help' was great fun but it wasn't our film. We were sort of guest stars. It was fun but basically as an idea for a film it was a bit wrong for us.
Paul McCartney

Given the choice between accomplishing something and just lying around, I'd rather lie around. No contest.
Eric Clapton

I decided to dedicate myself to explaining the Secret Language of Rock to the world.
A. J. Weberman, Dylanologist

Sometimes I feel like a robot.
Richard Carpenter

RICHARD CARPENTER

I feel like an actor when I'm on stage, rather than a rock artist. I very rarely have felt like a rock artist. I don't think that's much of vocation, being a rock 'n' roller.
David Bowie

I don't call myself a poet, because I don't like the word. I'm a trapeze artist.
Bob Dylan

People think the Beatles know what's going on. We don't. We're just doing it.
John Lennon

I don't know what's happening. I'm just the same as everyone else. I don't have a clue what's going on.
Van Morrison

We just get an idea for something, and then we try to do it.
Nick Mason, Pink Floyd

I didn't want to be a singer, I wanted to be an actor, and the only way I could stay in touch with the business was by bluffing.
Johnny Ray

I'm a true fairy.
Jobriath

We're the Oakland As of rock and roll. . On the field we can't be beat, but in the clubhouse, now that's another story.
Glenn Frey, Eagles

I must say I really don't like singing very much. I'm not really a good enough singer to really enjoy it, but I am getting into it little bit.
Mick Jagger

I have made it a point not to be oblique.
Lou Reed

Every year when I open a new diary, Easter Week is crossed off. My manager knows I'll be away camping then.
Cliff Richard

I'm thinking about entering politics, really doing it this time. I'd love to do it. But I haven't got the right wife.
Mick Jagger

I too slept with Jack Kennedy.
Bette Midler

Prancing around on stage is not the entire purpose of my life.
Grace Slick

AIN' THAT A FACT

Really, it was kind of like winning the football pools.
Van Morrison

Starvation in India doesn't worry me one bit. Not one iota, it doesn't man. And it doesn't worry you if you're honest. You just pose. You don't even know it exists. You've just seen the charity ads. You can't pretend to me that an ad reaches down into the depths of your soul and actually makes you feel more for these people than, for instance, you feel about getting a new car.
Paul McCartney

That was always something I despised.
Roger McGuinn on joining the LA Playboy Club, 1977

We're not the great thinkers of our time . . . we're as close to real thinking as Mary Whitehouse . . . just as naive and bigoted.
David Bowie

DAVID BOWIE/PHOTO BY MICK ROCK

If a guy does some great things, then even his down moments are interesting. You can't live your life without pressure periods.
Paul McCartney

I am my mother's boy, I am a mechanical toy.
Charles Manson

I needed a name in a hurry and I picked that one.
Bob Dylan

We were a band who made it very big, that's all. Our best work was never recorded.
John Lennon

It's a noise we make, that's all. You could be kind and call it music.
Mick Jagger

I'd rather be dead than singing 'Satisfaction' when I'm forty-five.
Mick Jagger

I'm probably the whitest singer in the world . . . but I can do this great feminine falsetto that sounds just like the way spade chicks sing.
Todd Rundgren

I'm paranoid about eating out of town tuna fish sandwiches, so I don't think I can discuss being a star intelligently.
Carly Simon

After all, I *am* the last white nigger.
Patti Smith

I'm not interested in my problems or attitudes, 'cos other people's are so much funnier.
Lou Reed

No-one's heart could be as wicked as mine. Many times I'm filled with hate or even murderous intent.
Tiny Tim

For a time we were in danger of becoming respectable.
Keith Richard

Just dig the noise and you've got our sound. We're musical primitives.
John Cale, Velvet Underground, 1966

I'm trying to be a singer without a dictionary and a poet not bound with shelves of books.
Bob Dylan

BRIAN JONES/PHOTO GERED MANKOWITZ

We've always had a wild image. We built ourselves on the fact. Groups like the Hollies envy our image.
Brian Jones

If I don't sing well live, it's simply 'cos I don't have functioning monitors.
Tom Verlaine

When Lou and I started the group, there was a basic understanding: it seemed more important to be different than immediately successful, to have a personality of our own, to have arrangements like Venus In Furs and to give concerts that were never the same.
John Cale, Velvet Underground, 1967

I've got to write songs. But if I had to do something else I'd like to be an osteopath. I'd like to cure arthritis and make people's bones work . . . that's if the world hasn't changed and everyone's a zombie. Because I think it's going that way. You gotta be a zombie and you gotta be cold.
Ray Davies

I never wanted to be a train driver, I wanted to be the best guitar player in the world.
Peter Frampton

I admire Patrick Moore.
Ray Davies

CARL PERKINS/PHOTO BY CHALKIE DAVIS

'Blue Suede Shoes' was the easiest song I ever wrote. Got up at 3.00 am when me and my wife Velda were living in a government project in Jackson, Tennessee. Had the idea in my head, seeing kids by the bandstand so proud of their new city shoes — you gotta be real poor to care about new shoes like I did — and that morning I went downstairs and wrote out the words on a potato sack. We didn't have any reason to have writing paper around.
Carl Perkins

JACK BRUCE/PHOTO BY EPOQUE LIMITED

I'm quite sure that if I wasn't in a group I'd be locked up. Probably in the nick for doing something I shouldn't.
Phil Lynott, Thin Lizzy

Being in Fleetwood Mac is more like being in group therapy.
Mick Fleetwood, 1977

Lawrence of Arabia was my only hero 'cos I thought it was real smooth his just coming out of England and leading the Arabs.
Joe Strummer, The Clash

We're not a great band. The musicianship is average, maybe even below, but in a year we're going to be the biggest band in the world. Two hundred million Americans out there don't appreciate subtleties. They want to be sledgehammered over the head with clear issues and no pussy-footing.
Gene Simmons, Kiss

I just happened to have the tape on the wrong way 'round. It just blew my mind. The voice sounds like an old Indian.
John Lennon on the first use of reverse tapes on 'Paperback Writer' 1966

I'm not kidding myself. My voice alone is just an ordinary voice. What people come to see is how I use it. If I stand still while I'm singing, I'm dead, man. I might as well go back to driving a truck.
Elvis Presley 1956

We're not trying to do anything except enjoy oursleves.
Willie Nelson

We chose the name because it represents something really cheap 'n' nasty.
Jeremy Valentine, The Cortinas

Being a good actor isn't easy. Being a man is even harder. I want to do both before I die.
James Dean

We just felt we had to change our names in order to make a mark — though mostly it was done just for fun.
Tom Verlaine (formerly Miller), Television

I've never wanted to be a household name . . . I'd rather be faceless, as it were.
Jack Bruce

PAYING THOSE DUES

If Muzak makes people happy . . . and contented in their environment, like air conditioning or a colour scheme — how can it not be good?
Umberto Bing Musciol Chairman of the Muzak Corporation

I'm working so hard, I'm working for the company. I'm working so hard to keep you in the luxury.
Mick Jagger and Keith Richard

The only guy who is honest is the guy who sings in the shower. Everyone else is a prostitute.
Kim Fowley

When you get in the record business someone gonna rip you anyway so that don't bother me. If you don't rip me, she gonna rip me, and if she don't rip me, he gonna rip me, so I'm gonna get ripped, so you don't be bothered by that, because people round you gonna rip you if they can.
Muddy Waters

It seems that all music has got caught up like selling jeans
Van Morrison

It's good to know karate. In this business you can never tell who is going to come up to you and do something to you.
Merrill Osmond

I probably made millions but I ain't never seen none of it.
Bo Diddley

To me, the music industry has got about as much meaning as a comic book
Van Morrison

It's been a hard day's night and I've been working like a dog.
John Lennon and Paul McCartney

It's a house we own together and there's no way of settling it unless we all decide to live in it.
John Lennon

You cannot reheat a soufflé.
Paul McCartney, on reuniting the Beatles.

I was born in 1947. I got my first guitar at ten. I toured with Chuck Berry for a year. I was with Herbie Hancock for a good count. I've paid my dues. They were, ah, $13 an hour, I believe.
Dan Hicks

My business interests are self-defence.
Frank Zappa

MUDDY WATERS

One has to completely humiliate oneself to be what the Beatles were, and that's what I resent.
John Lennon

If you're a writer, it's like making a sandwich, there's no great thing in it.
Donovan

Some people say that the power was green power. I must say that without green power you cannot make it, but you need love power to handle green power.
Little Richard

Money is basically green. Green is envy. Envy is headaches. Headaches are a drag. To me poor is poor, rich is rich. So what?
Cat Stevens

I don't play anything but the blues, but now I could never make no money on nothin' but the blues. That's why I wasn't interested in nothin' else.
Howlin' Wolf (Chester Burnett)

When they put it in my hand and I can see the green and count it, then I'll know it's mine.
Arthur Crudup

Every time a contract was brought out in front of us it would just be 'Hey, we're all brothers' . . . we were really into that whole thing. So we just signed.
Don Brewer, Grand Funk Railroad

By the mid-1970s, rock music will be San Francisco's fourth largest industry, led only by construction, finance insurance and manufacturing.
Michael Phillips, Vice President of the Bank of California, 1969

This agreement would not have been realised without the tireless efforts and Kissinger-like negotiating brilliance of Yoko Ono Lennon.
Allen Klein on the settlement of eight years of legal wrangles the Beatles' finances, 1977

In this Jubilee year I feel that it is only fitting that we should sign with a British company.
Mick Jagger on signing with EMI, 1977

Do you realise that 70 per cent of the jingles you hear on the air and on TV evolved from Brian Wilson's records.
Nick Venet, sometime producer of the Beach Boys

MARTIN BALIN

No bird ever signed a contract. No whale, no porpoise, no monkey . . . no iguana.
Martin Balin, explaining his refusal to sign a contract with the Jefferson Starship

Possession is nine tenths of the problem.
Dr. Winston O'Boogie

If Jesus Christ came to town he couldn't sell more tickets.
Wolfman Jack on the Rolling Stones' tour of America, 1972

Well the lines around my eyes are protected by a copyright law.
Mick Jagger and Keith Richard

I didn't want to leave the Beatles, the Beatles have left the Beatles. But no-one wants to be the one to say the party's over.
Paul McCartney

You never give me your money you only give me your funny paper. And in the middle of negotiations you break down.
John Lennon and Paul McCartney

Dear Sir Joe, From now on Allen Klein handles all my stuff.
Letter from John Lennon to Sir Joseph Lockwood, head of EMI, 1969

I'm not myself on tour. I'm a mechanical man. But I don't mind it, because I know it.
Gilbert O'Sullivan

PAYING THOSE DUES

When you're old enough to repay but young enough to sell.
Neil Young

If you drive a car I'll tax the seat. If you try to sit I'll tax the seat.
John Lennon and Paul McCartney

No commercial potential.
Frank Zappa on the original Mothers of Invention

We had the same fights we had when we were poor, except 'that's my tomato you're eating' became 'that's my limousine, get your ass out'.
Alice Cooper on the collapse of the band

You are on private property. There is no trespassing or loitering of any kind, by anyone under Section 8-610 BHMC. There is an armed guard on duty, trained dogs, in addition to the Bel-Air Patrol and a burglar service. All violators will be prosecuted to the full extent of the law and will be subject to fine or imprisonment and grave danger for entering private property. You are here at your own risk and are hereby advised to leave immediately.
Notice on Phil Spector's front gates

Q. Colonel Sanders, do you like hippies?
A. They eats chicken, don't they?

What people in America don't understand is that the music they heard was not Them but session men . . . I was forced to perform under these circumstances.
Van Morrison

For I don't care too much for money for money can't buy me love.
John Lennon and Paul McCartney

If you are a corporate executive trying to understand what is happening to youth today, you cannot afford to be without 'Rolling Stone'.
Ad for 'Rolling Stone' magazine

I don't want to make it sound like I'm rolling in money. I'm overdrawn, right. My current account is overdrawn. I get twenty-five dollars a day over here to pay for my food. Personally I have no money, but I've been told . . .
Peter Collins, Genesis

To reflect what's going on early enough to make a profit on it.
Dick Clark's manifesto for 'American Bandstand'

SOUNDS & FURIES

Rock and Roll is a means of pulling the White Man down to the level of the Negro. It is part of a plot to undermine the morals of the youth of our nation.
Secretary of the North Alabama White Citizens Council

Viewed as a social phenomenon, the current craze for rock and roll material is one of the most terrifying things to have ever happened to popular music. Musically speaking, of course, the whole thing is laughable.
Steve Race

Now in our popular music at least, we seem to be reverting to savagery and the most dramatic indication of this is the number of occasions in recent years when so-called concerts of rock 'n' roll have erupted into riots . . . these are no longer relaxed, normal kids. They will tell you they get a 'charge' out of rock 'n' roll. So do the kids who smoke marijuana and shoot 'H'.
Dmitri Tiomkin

I am the slime from your video, can't stop the slime, people, lookit me go.
Frank Zappa

I haven't seen any of Warhol's films, but of course they stink of titillation.
Cliff Richard

I may be old fashioned, but I never talk about toilet paper.
Tin Pan Alley songwriter, quoted in 'After the Ball' by Ian Whitcomb

Look at all the hate there is in Red China, then take a look around at Selma, Alabama.
P. F. Sloan

I'd rather see Bambi.
Loretta Lynn on 'Nashville'

England exploded didn't it? I don't know when.
Paul McCartney, 1965

If I had a child I wouldn't let him within a hundred miles of any American history, but would force him to sit for hours in front of video tapes of Johnny Carson.
Ian Anderson, Jethro Tull

Hitler did not change history — Hitler was history.
Bob Dylan

BOB DYLAN

JOHNNY CASH

We elected our man Nixon President, and if you don't stand behind him, get the hell out of the way so that I can stand behind him.
Johnny Cash

When Nixon was inaugurated I was driving nails. When Carter was elected I was playing the inauguration. That's got to tell you something.
James Talley

I'm not easily shocked, but the Twist shocked me . . . half Negroid, half Manhattan, and when you see it on its native heath, wholly frightening . . . I can't believe that London will ever go to quite these extremes . . . the essence of the Twist, the curious perverted heart of it, is that you dance it alone.
Beverley Nichols, 1962

Watergate is just an attack by the niggers and the Jews and the Commies on Nixon.
Attributed to Mike Curb, then President MGM Records

I shouted out 'Who killed the Kennedys?' When after all it was you and me.
Mick Jagger & Keith Richard

A scene more despicable than the Teddy Boy riots.
Anonymous journalist on the Rolling Stones at the Crawdaddy Club

John Lennon & Yoko Ono's services to the cause of furthering Communist aggression in Indo-China and weakening this country's will to resist will undoubtedly win for them Hanoi's highest honours.
Victor Lasky, syndicated US columnist

The underground suddenly leaps up in a horrified shriek when some spade hippie gets done, which is a terrible thing, but they never get uptight if some cop got done . . .gets crushed at a pop concert.
Keith Richard

I think Enoch Powell is the man. I'm all for him. This country is over-crowded. The immigrants should be sent home. That's it.
Rod Stewart

In the midst of ecstasy, after playing a song right for the first time, I would want my guitar to eat me alive.
Leo Kottke

The effect of rock and roll on young people is to turn them into devil worshippers, to stimulate self-expresssion through sex, to provoke lawlessness, impair nervous stability and destroy the sanctity of marriage. It is an evil influence on the youth of our country.
Reverend Albert Carter, Pentecostal Minister

We should send planes to Biafra and rescue all the people and then play at the airport as they come in.
Paul McCartney

I think Sir Winston Churchill was fantastic. The whole group were right cut up when he died.
Steve Marriott, Small Faces

I think one of the greatest dangers that faces people in this country is the tyrants who would come in and solve your crimes by putting a rock festival in every park and turning all the criminals free. And I think you'll lose your damned country.
Chief Ed Davies, Los Angeles Police Department

There's only been two big concerts for disasters, unless you count McGovern.
Writer Jacoba Atlas on the Rolling Stones Nicaragua Benefit

VAN MORRISON

NEIL YOUNG

Look at Mother Nature on the run in the Nineteen Seventies.
Neil Young

The Mersey Sound is the voice of 80,000 crumbling houses and 30,000 people on the dole.
Daily Worker, 1963

Their physical appearance, said my friend who is a Liverpool housewife, inspires frenzy. They look beat up and depraved in the nicest possible way.
Maureen Cleave writing on the Beatles, 'Evening Standard', 1963

I liked your advance party, but don't you think they could do with haircuts.
President Lyndon Johnson to Prime Minister Alec Douglas-Home, 1964

The Beatles, they're just a passing phase, symptoms of the uncertainty of the times and the confusion about us.
Billy Graham

Did you hear about the rock 'n' roll singers, got three or four Cadillacs, saying 'Power to the People' 'Dance to the music, wants you to pat him on the back'.
Van Morrison

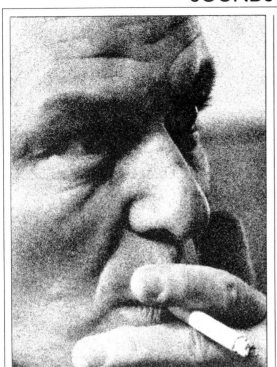

FRANK SINATRA

LOU REED

Rock 'n' roll is phony and false, and sung, written and played for the most part by cretinous goons.
Frank Sinatra, 1957

Give me your dirty love, like some tacky little pamphlet in your daddy's bottom drawer.
Frank Zappa

Handling Cherie Curry's ego is like having a dog urinate in your face.
Kim Fowley, producer of the Runaways

You can squirt me anywhere but in my face. You'll ruin my mascara.
Jackie Fox, the Runaways

You're the man who squats behind the man who works the soft machine.
Mick Jagger and Keith Richard

Sorry 'bout that sweat, honey, that's just holy water.
Little Richard

You may be a lover but you ain't no dancer.
John Lennon and Paul McCartney

I'm going to be the new J. Edgar Hoover of Washington. He used to know where all the dirt in Washington was, but now I'm the one who does.
A. J. Weberman, Dylanologist

Journalists are a species of foul vermin. I mean I wouldn't hire people like you to guard my sewer. Journalists are morons, idiots. I don't perform to idiots. Journalists are ignorant and stupid.
Lou Reed

Bass players have that problem — everything vibrates and pretty soon you can't jump up and down because you have to urinate.
Jackie Fox, The Runaways

I'm changing my image — I'm going to get my teeth fixed.
Keith Richard, 1974

I think people should be free at sex — they should draw the line at goats.
Elton John

The motorcycle black madonna, two-wheeled gypsy queen.
Bob Dylan

It's a dirty story of a dirty man, and his clinging wife doesn't understand.
John Lennon and Paul McCartney

Let's go watch Mick put on his makeup — that's always good for a laugh.
Ron Wood

Happiness Is A Warm Gun.
John Lennon

ERIC CLAPTON

RAY DAVIES

You know, English people have a very big thing toward a spade. Everybody in England still sort of thinks that spades have big dicks.
Eric Clapton

I just know that if I got mixed up in a love affair, then it would affect my work. It would ruin everything for me. That's why I'm denying myself.
Gilbert O'Sullivan

I want you to stop baby. I want you to walk back in your five inch spike heels that you got at Fredericks, same time you and your Mommy got that crotchless underwear last year for Christmas
Frank Zappa

I'm a little pimp with my hair gassed back. Pair of khaki pants and my shoe shined black. Gotta little lady walk that street tellin' all the boys that she can't be beat.
Frank Zappa

I wouldn't want *my* wife associating with us.
Charlie Watts, watching Mrs Margaret Trudeu posing for pictures with the Stones, March 1977

If God wants me to become a woman, then a woman I will become.
Mick Jagger, 1971

I'm not dumb but I can't understand why she walked like a woman and talked like a man.
Ray Davies

Some say your nose, some say your toes, but I think it's your *mind!*
Frank Zappa

I've got a girl named Boney Moronie, she's as skinny as a stick of macaroni.
Larry Williams

The Warden said 'Buddy, don't you be no square, if you can't find a partner use a wooden chair'.
Jerry Leiber and Mike Stoller

Your tricks with fruit were kinda cute, I'll bet you keep your pussy clean.
Mick Jagger and Keith Richard

In the morning the parking tickets were just like flags stuck on my windscreen.
Mick Jagger & Keith Richard

Everybody had a good year. Everybody let their hair down. Everybody pulled their socks up. Everybody put their foot down.
John Lennon

If we wanted to take Leary seriously, we should call LSD 'Let's Start Degeneracy'.
Harry J. Anslinger, Head of US Narcotics Squads

WORDS OF WISDOM

Death is a warm cloak. An old friend. I regard death as something that comes up on a roulette wheel every once in a while.
Gram Parsons

The act of creating is as integral part of life as going to the lavatory.
David Bowie

DAVID BOWIE

When you begin thinking you really *are* number one . . . that's when you begin to go nowhere.
Stevie Wonder

Everyone is in the best seat.
John Cage

I discovered the 'something' in 'nothing'.
Barbra Streisand

Life is just a vapour. You breathe in and what the heck.
Jerry Lee Lewis

If you can see farther than today or tomorrow, if you can see farther than that, then you're doing great.
Van Morrison

Time waits for no-one and it won't wait for you.
Mick Jagger and Keith Richard

'I'll let you be in my dreams if I can be in yours'. I said that.
Bob Dylan

To be honest, y'know, I don't have any hopes for the future and I just hope to have enough boots to be able to change them. That's all, really. It doesn't boil down to anything more than that. If it did, I certainly would tell you.
Bob Dylan

Me and my brother were talking to each other about what makes a man a man, was it brains, was it brawn, or the month you were born. We just couldn't understand.
Pete Townshend

That's what it all comes down to. Whether or not, when the time comes, you decide to jump in the pot.
Arlo Guthrie

KEITH RICHARD/PHOTO BY GERED MANKOWITZ

I'll just keep on rocking and hope for the best.
Keith Richard

Everybody's got a different musical note . . . What am I? I think I'm F-sharp.
Donovan

I'm not really interested in music. Music is just a means of creating a magical state.
Robert Fripp, King Crimson

How Can You Be In Two Places At Once, When You're Not Anywhere At All?
Firesign Theatre, album title

I reckon extremes augment themselves. A quiet sleep makes for an active day, starving makes for an enjoyable meal, and hunting makes for great rock 'n' roll.
Ted Nugent

Most people wouldn't know good music if it came up and bit them in the ass.
Frank Zappa

The words of the prophets are written on the subway walls and tenement halls.
Paul Simon

We are all the same. No-one's on any higher level than anybody else. We've all got it within us for whatever we want to grasp for.
Bob Dylan

Never underestimate people's ability to not know when they're in pain.
Art Garfunkel

Don't let your mouth write no cheque your tail can't cash.
Bo Diddley

Everyone in the world is getting fucked one way or another. All you can do is see that you aren't fucking them directly.
Paul Kantner

You can only apologise for so much.
Steven Stills

You can be wrong and you don't have to say you're sorry.
Allen Klein

I'm a firm believer that people find out what they want to find out.
Don McLean

JONI MITCHELL

The light poured in like butterscotch and stuck to all my senses.
Joni Mitchell

When you put six ducks and a rat on stage, the rat's gonna stand out.
Grace Slick

Sometimes you got to take a chance and do something that everyone thinks is crazy . . . Everyone should do that once in his life.
Arlo Guthrie

Holes in my confidence, holes in the knees of my jeans.
Paul Simon

I would like to persuade the audience not to wear any blue denim . . . I don't enjoy the sky or the sea because of this Levi character.
Ian Anderson, Jethro Tull

Peace ran like a river through the city.
Paul Simon

We're captive on the carousel of time, can't return we can only look behind.
Joni Mitchell

I see my life come shining from the West down to the East. Any day now, any way now, I shall be released.
Bob Dylan

I'm happy when life's good and when it's bad I cry. I got values but I don't know how or why.
Pete Townshend

A Hard Rain's A-Gonna Fall
Bob Dylan

It is also nice that we share the air. No matter how far apart we are, the air links us.
Yoko Ono

Chemistry is applied theology.
Augustus Stanley Owsley III

If a man can bridge the gap between life and death. I mean, if he can live on after he's died, then maybe he was a great man.
James Dean

If people want to make war, they should make a colour war, and paint each other's cities up in the night in pinks and greens.
Yoko Ono

Our goal is always to be successful and rich, but that goal doesn't imply that we're going to be happier and more generous people, so why do we want that goal?
Harry Chapin

I'd like to act as a catalyst for using rock music and technological electronic music in a positive, healthy and beneficial way. This is the key to solving the world's problems — I think.
Steve Hillage

Take what you can use and let the rest go by.
Ken Kesey

It's not the size of the ship, it's the size of the waves.
Little Richard

It's all soul.
Junior Wells

The faster we go, the rounder we get.
Grateful Dead

In and out of circles so much time we seem to waste. To make our plans and find that all our plans have been erased.
Neil Sedaka

Fuzzy hair is radiant. My hair is electric. It picks up *all* the vibrations.
Jimi Hendrix

WORDS OF WISDOM

We are stardust, we are golden and we got to get ourselves back to the garden.
Joni Mitchell

Well we all shine on like the stars and the moon and the sun.
John Lennon

I am the Chrome Dinette.
Frank Zappa

One man's ceiling is another man's floor.
Paul Simon

Music, a really heavy vibration, says a lot more than a million words could in eternity say. As far as really holy sounds go.
Carl Wilson, Beach Boys

I want to get a seeing eye lion, so no-one will refuse us entrance anywhere.
José Feliciano

I haven't really got a home anywhere. The earth's my home. I don't want to put down roots in case I get restless.
Jimi Hendrix

He ain't heavy, he's my brother.
Bobby Scott

I'm one too many mornings and a thousand miles behind.
Bob Dylan

It's hard to bullshit the ocean. It's not listening, you know what I mean.
David Crosby

THE BEACH BOYS

JOHN LENNON & YOKO ONO/PHOTO BY RICHARD DILELLO

If the butterflies in your stomach die, send yellow death announcements to your friends.
Yoko Ono

Make a bigger place in the universe for your head to live in and it will grow to fill the space.
David Crosby

I don't think Jimi committed suicide in the conventional way. He just decided to exit when he wanted to.
Eric Burdon

Having reached the end of space, you look across the wall and there's more space.
Paul McCartney

It is sad that the air is the only thing we share. No matter how close we get to each other, there is always air between us.
Yoko Ono

Music might not stop atomic bombs, but it would help if positive, globally related ideas were put over on a large scale by the media.
Steve Hillage

So the thing is, if you really want to get it permanently, you have got to do it, you know . . . be healthy, don't eat meat, keep away from those night-clubs and *meditate*.
George Harrison

Your wig steers the gig.
Lord Buckley

You've got all the time in the world. What's the rush, buddy? Take-It-Easy, that's the play, it's bound to sweeten the way.
Mezz Mezzrow

If you get to it, and you can't do it — well, there you jolly well are, aren't you.
Lord Buckley

The whole universe is your home if you can get big enough to live in it. It's there. It doesn't care. You can come out and live there. You just have to get big enough.
David Crosby

The finest sensibilities of the age are convulsed with pain. That means a change is at hand.
Leonard Cohen

STRUTTIN' YOUR STUFF

One of the first principles in everybody's mind is to put the orgasm back into rock.
Mick Farren, Deviants

I think pop music has done more for oral intercourse than anything else that ever happened, and vice verse.
Frank Zappa

Keep on churnin' till the butter comes.
Wynonie Harris

Am I clean? Am I clean? Am I spotless? Am I pure???
P. J. Proby, stage exhortation

Don't forget, the penis is mightier than the sword.
Screamin' Jay Hawkins

I try never to be alone with a beautiful woman. Because when I'm alone, the devil in me becomes dangerous.
Tiny Tim

A lot of tunes in the guise of romanticism have mainly fucking behind them.
Randy Newman

Rock 'n' Roll meant fucking originally. That's what it originally meant, which I don't think is a bad idea. Let's bring it back again.
Waylon Jennings

I went out for coffee and some papers and I didn't come back.
John Lennon, on his temporary separation from Yoko Ono

I always thought the hoods, the bad kids, were more mature than the football players. The good kids would talk about getting fucked, but the Lairds, they got *laid*.
Marty Balin

Self-denial is a great thing.
Gilbert O'Sullivan

CAPTAIN BEEFHEART/PHOTO BY BYRON NEWMAN

I've been wearing black leather all my life.
Bob Dylan

But don't you feel a little guilty when someone catches you looking at one of those fold-out pictures in the 'men's magazines'. Don't you blush slightly when you're discovered reading 'My Awful Confessions' or some mag like that. Don't you hesitate to mention that you saw 'I Was a Teenage Sexpot' at the movie last night? I *hope* you hesitate and blush and feel guilty — if so, there's still hope for you.
Pat Boone

Give me the enchilada with the pickle sauce shoved up between a donkey's ass until he can't come any more!
Frank Zappa

Why Don't We Do It In The Road?
John Lennon and Paul McCartney

Chicks were born to give you fever, Fahrenheit or Centigrade.
John Davenport and Eddie Cooley

The best diet for the road is soup for lunch and candy for supper. It keeps the weight off and you're speeding on all that sugar by showtime.
Paul Stanley, Kiss

Come on baby take a chance with us and meet me by the back of the blue bus.
Jim Morrison

Women like long-necked bottles, and a big head on the beer.
Captain Beefheart (Don Van Vliet)

You thought you were a clever girl giving up your social whirl but you can't come back, be the first in line. You're obsolete my baby.
Mick Jagger and Keith Richard

I remember you in Hemlock Row in 1956. You were a faggy little leather boy with a smaller piece of stick. You were a lashing, smashing hunk of man, your sweat shines sweet and strong. Your organ's working perfectly but there's a part that's not screwed on.
Mick Jagger and Keith Richard

Only thirteen and she knows how to nasty.
Frank Zappa

JIM MORRISON

BONNIE BRAMLETT

You know, they say men use women as sex objects. Hey, man, if a chick gets used as a sex object, that's her fault. I don't get used as a sex object.
Bonnie Bramlett

I got nipples on my titties big as the end of my thumb. I got somethin' between my legs'll make a dead man come. Oooh, daddy-baby, won't you shave 'em dry, ooh!
Lucille Brogan

Now my hair is nappy and I don't wear no clothes of silk but the cow that's black and ugly, has often got the sweetest milk.
Sara Martin

In a carefully prepared loving LSD session a woman will inevitably have several hundred orgasms.
Timothy Leary

I whipped off her bloomers and stiffened my thumb and applied rotation on her sugar plum.
Frank Zappa

The maid she's French, she's got no sense she's from the Crazy Horse. And when she strips the chauffeur flips, the footman's eyes get crossed.
Mick Jagger and Keith Richard

Wearing a face that she keeps in a jar by the door.
John Lennon and Paul McCartney

Make me grow Brainiac fingers but with more hair
Frank Zappa

Girls will be boys and boys will be girls. It's a mixed up, muddled up, shook-up world.
Ray Davies

JOHN WAYNE

Well, there are three things men can do with women: love them, suffer for them, or turn them into literature.
Stephen Stills

If a guy wants to wear his hair down to his ass, I'm not revolted by it. But I don't look at him and say 'Now there's a fella I'd like to spend next winter with'.
John Wayne

We do love songs of every description. 'Venus In Furs' is just a different kind of love song.
Sterling Morrison, Velvet Underground, 1966

I've been 105 pounds for ten years. Before that less. That's why I had to fantasise about Arthur Rimbaud. I wasn't exactly a dream date. I eat all the time. I love to eat. But with this manic energy I burn it off as I'm swallowing.
Patti Smith

A pair of tits like that and you tend to forget she has a voice.
Roger Gover, producer of Barbi Benton

I've got plenty of nothing, and nothing's plenty for me. I got my hand, I got my dick, I got my fantasy.
Ken Weaver, The Fugs

A woman is like a dresser — some man always goin' through her drawers.
Anon, Vintage Blues

No girl can really sustain an album's worth of material, though Tammy Wynette and Dolly Parton come close.
Tim Rice

Men have an unusual talent for making a bore out of everything they touch.
Yoko Ono

The only position for women in SNCC is prone.
Stokely Carmichael, 1966

GOD ONLY KNOWS

BOB MARLEY

Sometime Jah show you thing before they happen. Like before them go shoot up de place, me have a dream say me hear plenty gunshot. And the same thing happen. Vision, yeah!
Bob Marley

Either be hot or cold. If you are lukewarm, the Lord will spew you forth from His mouth.
Jerry Lee Lewis.

Life is so short and you want to see everyone be happy. I feel like I'm a prophet to help people. I was put here to teach the goodness to people.
Little Richard

I think God is groovy. He had a great publicity agent.
P. J. Proby

Cowboys and Jews have a common bond — they are the only two groups of people to wear their hats indoors and attach a certain amount of importance to it.
Richard F. 'Kinky' Friedman

May the Baby Jesus shut your mouth and open your mind.
Motto of the Family Dog organisation, San Francisco, 1966

To Know Him Is To Love Him
Song Title by Phil Spector

So I say that we're God's bouquet. We're just like the rose, the lilies, the sunflowers and the medallion.
Little Richard

You don't want to walk and talk about Jesus, just wanna see his face.
Mick Jagger and Keith Richard

If my God came into the room, I'd be awed obviously, but I don't think I'd be humble. I might cry, but I know he'd dig me like mad.
Marc Bolan

Mrs. Whitehouse is ten years ahead of her time.
Cliff Richard

The music I played in church on religious occasions is the only music that interests me.
Little Richard, 1959

It's hard to be cosmic verbally, but the whole point of my album is that *you* are the Messiah.
Ray Manzarek

Clean living keeps me in shape. Righteous thoughts are my secret. And New Orleans home cooking.
Fats Domino

It would be nice to publish alternate universes.
Jerry Garcia

That deaf, dumb and blind kid sure plays a mean pinball.
Pete Townshend

Christ died for somebody's sins, but not mine.
Patti Smith

Pop is the perfect religious vehicle. It's as if God has come down to earth and seen all the ugliness that was being created and chosen pop to be the great force for love and beauty.
Donovan

I don't aim to let this fame business get me. God gave me a voice. If I turned against God I'd be ruined.
Elvis Presley

ELVIS PRESLEY

I'm a conductor of revivals. The only minister in the whole package. Little Richard, the evangelist.
Little Richard

They paved paradise and put up a parking lot, with a pink hotel, a boutique, and a swinging hot spot.
Joni Mitchell

I am 100 per cent Christian and everything I do is with my religion in mind.
Cliff Richard

Satya Sai Baba is not my guru, we're just good friends.
George Harrison

What is evil? I don't know how much people think of Mick as the Devil or as just a good rock performer. There are black musicians who think we are acting as unknown agents of Lucifer and others who think we are Lucifer. Everybody's Lucifer.
Keith Richard

Jesus raised the dead, but who will raise the living?
Tom Rapp

Everybody's talking about Bagism, Shagism, Dragism, Madism, Ragism, Ragism, Thisism, Thatism . . .
John Lennon and Paul McCartney

Well, first of all, God is a woman. Well, you take it from there.
Bob Dylan on religion, 1965

If Jesus Christ came back today, he and I would get into our brown corduroys and go to the nearest jean store and overturn the racks of blue denim. Then we'd get crucified in the morning.
Ian Anderson, Jethro Tull

Anyone who thinks a Christian is soft can think again.
Cliff Richard

Janis bought a stone for Bessie Smith, but she forgot she hadn't paid for her own.
Dory Previn

See me, feel me, touch me, heal me.
Pete Townshend

As long as I gaze on Waterloo sunset, I am in paradise.
Ray Davies

WAYNE COUNTY/PHOTO BY JILL FURMANOVSKY

Decadence rules, it's so lovely, so unlimited, so natural. If Jesus Christ came back again and took me for a beer I'd never change. I mean, he was one hell of a strange boy himself.
Wayne County

God is a concept by which we measure our pain.
John Lennon

And the Lord said, and the Lord said 'I burn down your cities, how blind you must be. I take from you your children and you say "How blessed are we". You must all be crazy to put your faith in me. That's why I love mankind'.
Randy Newman

I live by the Bible and I read in it that we should not worry about such things, that death comes when and where it wishes and that we must have faith and wait.
Cliff Richard

All the gurus and things you pick up one week because the TV is boring or your old lady is pissed and then you drop them.
Arlo Guthrie

God let me come along at this time.
Elvis Presley

Religion is a big help I think, if you can buy.
Randy Newman

Well, I don't know, but I've been told the streets of heaven are paved with gold.
Bob Dylan

MICK JAGGER/PHOTO BY MICHAEL PUTLAND

There is another area that doesn't encompass God or the Devil. That's the area to go.
Mick Jagger, in the film 'Performance'

I feel I ought to have a guru so I can talk about some evangelical message that people feel is significant.
Manfred Mann

Everything that God said in prophecies have to come true. It's just that some people are more aware of it, more aware of the spiritual part of life.
Bob Marley

This is not a true and accurate portrayal of the life of Jesus Christ, Son of God. For a true and accurate account, please read the Bible.
Postscript added to the film of 'Jesus Christ Superstar', ordered by the Protestant Church authorities in Singapore.

Christianity will go. It will go. It will vanish and shrink. I needn't argue about that. I'm right and will be proved right. We are more popular than Jesus now. I don't know which will go first — rock and roll or Christianity. Jesus was alright but his disciples were thick and ordinary.
John Lennon

But I can't think for you, you'll have to decide whether Judas Iscariot had God on his side.
Bob Dylan

You know, if God showed up tomorrow and said What do you want to do, yeah, if he said Do you want to be President? No. Do you want to be in politics? No. Do

you want to be a lawyer? No. What do you want? I want to be a rhythm guitar player.
Lou Reed

If like they say they ain't no God, but then it be just one man aginst another, the way I see it, maybe I just better watch out for myself.
Lightnin' Hopkins

I find myself evil. I believe in the Devil as much as God. You can use either one to get things done.
Peter Criss, Kiss

All the lonely people, where do they all come from? All the lonely people, where do they all belong?
John Lennon and Paul McCartney

We gotta send Santa Claus back to the Rescue Mission.
Frank Zappa

The career of James Dean has not ended. It has just begun. And God Himself is directing the production.
Pastor Xan Harvey, eulogising James Dean

People that use God as a weapon should be amputated upon.
Bob Dylan

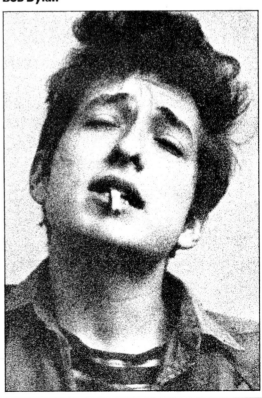

BOB DYLAN

PAIN IN MY HEART

I can't feel strongly, I get so numb.
David Bowie

I believe that in America if ever there's a real revolution Andy Warhol will sponsor it and it will have fake bombs and you throw them and a little thing comes out and goes 'Pow!'.
Joe MacDonald

You are all a bunch of fucking idiots. Your faces are pressed into the shit of the world. Take your fucking friend and love him. Do you want to see my *cock*?!
Jim Morrison, shortly prior to exposing himself on stage.

Everybody has to have a little bottle of neuroses to sprinkle on people.
Captain Beefheart (Don Van Vliet)

Plastic boots and plastic hat and you think you know where it's at.
Frank Zappa

I go down to John's place to play with his toys and sometimes he comes down here to play with mine.
Ringo Starr

After a certain point, what the hell's so great about lying around in the mud.
Anonymous festival goer, quoted in 'Rolling Stone' magazine

Folk singing is just a bunch of fat people.
Bob Dylan

You think we look pretty good together, you think my shoes are made of leather but I'm a substitute for another guy, I look pretty tall but my heels are high.
Pete Townshend

If you get rich singing badly about society, you can't really sing badly about it any more.
Amiri Baraka (Leroi Jones)

This country places a tremendous priority on being successful, but there is a tremendous lack of people who are good at what they do.
Paul Simon

I don't think I've done anything decadent in the last six months.
David Bowie

It's bloody difficult staying in bed for seven days when you are perfectly healthy.
John Lennon

Do you love it? Do you hate it? There it is the way you made it.
Frank Zappa

There's a lot to be said against San Francisco and its love people, and a lot more to be said for the New York hard-core degenerate.
Paul Morrissey

When you do ten songs in a movie they can't all be good songs. Anyway, I got tired of singing to turtles.
Elvis Presley on his 1970 Las Vegas Return

I don't really respect Jeff Beck and Jimmy Page.
Pete Townshend

We've got absolutely no intention of ending up like The Tremeloes.
Keith Moon

I think for the life span he's lasted, Chuck Berry's productivity has been nil, more or less.
Elton John

Hey, hey Woody Guthrie, I wrote you a song 'bout a funny old world that's a-comin' along.
Bob Dylan

Nothing happened in the Sixties except that we all dressed up.
John Lennon

People were just asking for it. All those nude, fat people. They had victims faces.
Keith Richard on the murder at Altamont

I've had enough of watching scenes of schizophrenic, egocentric paranoiac prima-donnas.
John Lennon

I have a terrible feeling that I'll wake up on my thirtieth birthday and my looks will have gone.
Marianne Faithfull

Have my best days gone? Truthfully I have to answer yes.
Phil Spector

That bullshit about the people's music, man, where's that at? I wasn't any people that sat with me when I learned to play the guitar. If the people think that way, they can play their own fucking music.
Jerry Garcia

The sunshine bores the daylights out of me.
Mick Jagger

How does it feel to be on your own, with no direction home, like a complete unknown, like a rolling stone?
Bob Dylan

Well the change it had to come, we knew it all along, we liberated rock from the four-minute song.
Pete Townshend

Where have all the flowers gone? Young girls picked them every one.
Pete Seeger

Did you ever hear about the Great Deception? Where the plastic revolutionaries take the money and run.
Van Morrison

The pen is mightier than the sword but no match for a gun.
Leiber and Stoller

No good times, no bad times, there's no times at all, just the 'New York Times'.
Paul Simon

Where have you gone Joe diMaggio? A nation turns its lonely eyes to you.
Paul Simon

Yes, I wish that for just one time you could stand inside my shoes. You'd know what a drag it is to see you.
Bob Dylan

I'm interested in anything about revolt, disorder, chaos, especially activity that seems to have no meaning.
Jim Morrison

See the new boss, same as the old boss.
Pete Townshend

While stars sit in bars and decide what they're drinking. They drop by to die, 'cos it's faster than sinking.
Neil Young

Generation to generation, nothing changes in Bohemia.
Nik Cohn

You like people? I hate them . . . screw them, I don't need them . . . of course, I need them . . . to grow potatoes.
Jim Morrison

What have you got to lose? Every way you look at it you lose.
Paul Simon

When you've made your million, when you've cut your monsters, when your peak has been passed . . . what happens next? What about the fifty years before you die?
Nik Cohn

You've got to watch your mind all the time, or you'll awaken and find a strange picture on your press.
Lord Buckley

All is loneliness.
Moondog

All the people I've known who were fabulous have either died, flipped or gone to India.
Lou Reed

There ain't no life nowhere.
Jimi Hendrix

Along we go, we play through our LP tracks and we do our joke announcements, and we do our commercial numbers and we do our movements. And then it comes to the end and we do 'My Generation' and we fucking smash everything up.
Pete Townshend, 1968

PETE TOWNSHEND

RY COODER

It really bothers me that a twerp like Jagger can parade around and convince everyone that he's Satan.
Ry Cooder

It will give me great pleasure to tell the public that Mick Jagger is not God Junior.
Bill Graham, promoter

Bill Graham may be an asshole, but he gave me some of the best years of my life.
Anonymous tribute sent into KSAN Radio, San Francisco

David Cassidy is like a male Ann-Margaret.
Anonymous, quoted in 'Rolling Stone' Magazine

Mick Jagger moves like a parody between a majorette girl and Fred Astaire.
Truman Capote

Mick Jagger — isn't he that motorcycle rider?
Gerald Ford

He may be the Prince of Darkness to you, but over here he's just one of the fellas.
Lillian Roxon's lead for a piece on the Rolling Stones 1972 tour of the U.S.A.

That cunt is a great entertainer.
Bill Graham on Mick Jagger

Mick Jagger loves to humiliate people, but he was nice to me because he needed the music.
Ry Cooder

The Rolling Stones are on a really bad trip. They're on a nonsence trip. Their trip is as disgusting as Nixon's.
Steve Miller

I'll never be a star like Jimi Hendrix or Bob Dylan. I figured out why — because I tell the truth. If they want to know who I am, they ask me and I tell them.
Janis Joplin

Quite simply, I personally feel that the Stones are the world's best rock 'n' roll band.
Pete Townshend

When I get up in the morning I listen to Vivaldi and 'Marvin Gaye's Greatest Hits'.
Mick Jagger

Mick Jagger is more of a showman than I am. And I'm more of a singer than he is. That's not a put-down of either of us.
Rod Stewart

Mick Jagger is the perfect pop star. There's nobody more perfect than Jagger. He's rude, he's ugly-attractive, he's brilliant. The Rolling Stones are the perfect pop group — they don't give a shit.
Elton John

I'm tired of Janis Joplin stories. It's always the same damn thing.
'Esquire' Magazine editor

None of them can follow me, including Tom Jones. I cut his ass down too. And he knows it, 'cos I taught him what he knows. Love him like a brother, but I don't want him to forget who the old master is.
Jerry Lee Lewis

Sonny and Cher are a drag. A guy gets kicked out of a restaurant and he went home and wrote a song about it.
Bob Dylan

You'd think he had the decency to collect my stuff the way I collect him.
A. J. Weberman, Dylanologist, on discovering some of his own writings while investigating Bob Dylan's garbage

If you look at Bob Dylan's career, his big thing in life was not to play the Fillmore, but to be a hit in Tin Pan Alley and make money.
Paul Morrissey, Andy Warhol's movie producer

Buddy Holly always struck me as the type more likely to be found serving in a hamburger bar or delivering the soft drinks.
Paul Anka

He could be a drunken sot, a kind of Keats, a rock 'n' roll star who was so fucking famous it was unbelievable, and his private idol could be Fritz the Cat.
Michael McLure on Jim Morrison

Thank God for the Beatles, they showed us a trick or two. Cut them down like wheat before the sickle.
Jerry Lee Lewis

How did I decide to form the Byrds? I saw the Beatles, that's why. Bang!
Roger McGuinn

The greatest composers since Beethoven.
Richard Buckle, in the 'Sunday Times'

I love Beethoven, especially the poems.
Ringo Starr

You know, people like the Jefferson Airplane, Grateful Dead, all those people are just the most untalented bores that ever came up . . I mean, can you take Grace Slick seriously? It's a joke, it's a joke. The kids are being hyped.
Lou Reed

Oh is he more, too much more than a pretty face? (I don't think so).
David Essex

DAVID ESSEX

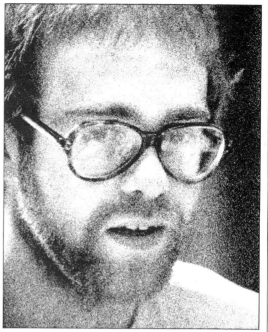

I don't think he was ever born to be a rock 'n' roll star. He was probably born to be chairman of Watford Football Club, and now he's beginning to look like the Chairman of Watford Football Club as well.
Rod Stewart on Elton John, 1977

My greatest influences are the Beatles and Tchaikovsky.
Roy Wood, Wizzard

I was into the technique of mastering the impression of John Lennon's voice and Bob Dylan's voice and getting it down the middle.
Roger McGuinn, 1965

There was not another sonofabitch in the country who could sing until Dylan came along. Everyone else was singing like a damned faggot.
Rambling Jack Elliott

It's really hard to follow Bob.
George Harrison after Dylan's appearance at the Concert for Bangla Desh, August 1971

Jimi Hendrix' head was in the same place mine is. I understand him and his music completely.
Duane Thomas, running back for the Washington Redskins

I don't even think of Hendrix as black. Hendrix is Hendrix.
Alvin Lee

I am capable of being a rock 'n' roll star and the Chairman of Watford Football Club and I sell more records throughout the world than Rod Stewart. Anyway, he should stick to grave-digging, 'cos that's where he belongs, six feet under.
Elton John's reply to Rod Stewart, 1977

I'm a John Denver freak. I don't give a shit that he looks like a fucking turkey.
Grace Slick

Janis Joplin . . . a kind of mixture of Leadbelly, a steam engine, Calamity Jane, Bessie Smith, an oil derrick and rotgut bourbon, funneled into the Twentieth Century somewhere between El Paso and San Francisco.
'Cashbox' Magazine

I have made up the boys and they have poor skins, fairly spotty too. They needed very careful makeup.
Carol Perry, BBC makeup girl, recalling the Osmonds

I got the feeling that Janis was the wrong person in the wrong place and she got treated the wrong way.
Joe MacDonald

I don't like the Beatles, I think they stink, man. I never did like them.
Jerry Lee Lewis

I'll scratch your back and you knife mine.
John Lennon

I'd be tickled pink if I could get away with the kind of suave comedy Cary Grant does. I've seen a lot of his films and I think he's really great.
Cliff Richard

Gram Parsons is the best because he's the skinniest.
Phil Ochs

Having played with other musicians, I don't even think the Beatles were that good.
George Harrison

If you see George Harrison, you can tell him I think he's a load of old rope.
Cliff Richard

I'd prefer to be known as the female Elvis Presley — he's the greatest showman since Liberace.
Shirley Bassey

I want to become a good actor, because you can't build a whole career on just singing. Look at Frank Sinatra. Until he added acting to singing he found himself slipping down hill.
Elvis Presley, 1959

The Velvet Underground's songs should be sung by Frank Sinatra — he would sing them beautifully.
Nico

Mancini is a God-given talent. And so is Brian Wilson.
Murray Wilson

Those freaks was right when they said you was dead. The one mistake you made was in your head . . . the sounds you make is muzak to my ears, you must have learnt something in all those years.
John Lennon

Paul's really writing for a fourteen-year-old auidence now.
George Harrison

If you want to hear pretentiousness, just listen to John Lennon's 'Imagine'. All that 'possessions' crap.
Lou Reed

I'd join a band with John Lennon any day, but I wouldn't join a band with Paul McCartney.
George Harrison

The Jefferson Airplane is the only rock group in the world for me.
Jean-Luc Godard

Tina Turner is a female James Brown.
Stevie Wonder

The newspapers said 'She's gone to his head. They look just like two Gurus in drag'.
John Lennon and Paul McCartney

NICO

PAUL MCCARTNEY

Dylan gets on my nerves. If you were at a party with him I think you'd tell him to shut up.
Lou Reed

Richard Burton would play Captain Pissgums and we'd get Liz Taylor to play the dyke.
Ken Kesey

Dolly Parton's just kind of a Southern magnolia blossom that floats on the breeze.
Linda Ronstadt

As a person I can't sing Dylan's nasty, hateful songs. I can appreciate the honesty of them, and melodically they're good, but I can't sing them.
Joan Baez, 1969

I have no respect for Jim Morrison. I didn't even feel sorry for him when he died.
Lou Reed

Jimmy Page did play tambourine on our first record. It was very good tambourine and he's a very good musician.
Ray Davies

I am unable to see in Dylan anything other than a youth of mediocre talent. Only a completely non-critical audience, nourished on the watery pap of pop music could have fallen for such tenth-rate drivel.
Ewan MacColl, writing in Sing Out, 1965

They think they know the real Jim Reeves from a bit of wax. This 'Gentleman Jim' bit that suddenly came about — the perfect gentleman — he wasn't like this at all . . . The other side of his character is better left unsaid, the fans don't want to hear it.
David Bussey, secretary of the Jim Reeves fan club.

Whether or not he decides to join forces with the human race, Dylan's a genius.
Joan Baez, 1969

She was like a Mum to us.
John Lennon on meeting Queen Elizabeth II

Frank Zappa couldn't write a decent song if you gave him a million and a year on an island in Greece.
Lou Reed

The queen housewife of rock.
Kim Fowley on Helen Reddy

He stole my music but he gave me my name.
Muddy Waters on Mick Jagger

The Beatles have to be the most incredible songwriters ever — just amazingly talented. I don't think people realize how sad it is that the Beatles broke up.
Lou Reed

Four cats with a passion.
Nicholas Ray, director of Rebel Without a Cause', on Television

I don't believe in Beatles.
John Lennon

Bobby Dylan says what a lot of people my age feel but cannot say.
Joan Baez

I started off writing instrumentals. My idol at that time was Hank B. Marvin, Cliff Richard's guitar player.
Neil Young

I've always seen David as a building. I visualise him as a building. Something like the Pan Am building on Park Avenue.
Tony DeFries, David Bowie's manager

I like Dylan's whole attitude. The way he dresses, the way he doesn't given a damn, the way he sings discords and plays discords. The way he sends up everything.
George Harrison

The Sex Pistols sent me these great day-glo lime green ankle socks. I'm wearing them now.
Patti Smith

Frank Zappa is probably the single most untalented person I've heard in my life. He's two-bit, pretentious, academic and he can't play his way out of anything. He can't play rock 'n' roll, because he's a loser. And that's why he dresses so funny. He's not happy with himself and I think he's right.
Lou Reed

Woody Guthrie, frankly, was a genius writer, but Guthrie couldn't hold Seeger's socks as a human being.
Harry Chapin

DAVID CASSIDY

He was like a young beautiful green fern, unfurling .. now he's grown into a pliable, firm plant.
Gloria Stavers, editor of 'Sixteen Magazine' on David Cassidy

Alice Cooper are the worst, most disgusting side of rock music.
Lou Reed

I don't know John Lennon. The last thing he said to me was 'Fuck off'.
Ray Davies

Pete Townshend is . . . so talentless, and as a lyricist he's so profoundly untalented and, you know, philosophically boring to say the least . . .
Lou Reed

THE WILD AND THE WOOLY

If you're a rock musician you don't have to put on any airs and pretend to be all grown up.
Pete Townshend

Q: Do you wear wigs?
A: If we do, they must be the only ones with real dandruff.
John Lennon

Spiders are a gas. I mean, they must be, or they wouldn't exist, would they? So they must be a gas. Just because I don't like them, it doesn't mean they aren't a gas.
Ronnie Lane, Small Faces

Probably one word will always be akin to the Beach Boys, which is surfing.
Brian Wilson

I'm so happy. It's so nice to go with a man whose clothes you can wear.
Britt Ekland

Q: Why do you wear all those rings on your fingers?
A: Because I can't get them through my nose.
Ringo Starr

RINGO STARR

So I took out my hatchet and chopped the Holiday Inn room to bits. The television. The chairs. The cupboard doors. The bed. It happens all the time.
Keith Moon

People don't want to talk to you, y'know, if you're throwing up. Particularly if you're doing it in their room. If I throw up in my room, it's alright.
Grace Slick

A relationship with animals is so real, somehow. It's all too easy to get carried away with being in a rock group.
Robert Plant

The monkeys stand for honesty, giraffes are insincere, and the elephants are kindly but they're dumb.
Paul Simon

We were the first band to vomit in the bar and find the distance to the stage too far.
Pete Townshend

Those places were so tough you had to show your razor and puke twice before they'd let you in.
Ronnie Hawkins

We need to have to carry the Arkansas credit card — a syphon hose and a five-gallon can.
Ronnie Hawkins

Those of you in the cheaper seats, clap your hands. Those of you in the more expensive ones rattle your jewellery.
John Lennon

What I like doing most of all is sticking pins into people's buttocks, be they musical or physical pins. Very firmly into people's buttocks and cause great anguish and leaping up and down.
Jonathan King, bubblegum entrepreneur

I dislike commercial pop because I cannot accept the intention behind it — I don't get those vibrations from Stravinsky.
Frank Zappa

You can do anything you want at Alice's Restaurant.
Alro Guthrie

Give me a stringbean, I'm a hungry man.
Bob Dylan

I don't think interviews oughta be done unless you've just driven a Rolls Royce into a Holiday Inn pool.
Grace Slick

Yes, yes, the Mascara Snake, fast and bulbous.
Captain Beefheart

And of course, Harry the Horse dances the waltz.
John Lennon and Paul McCartney

Billy was a mountain, Ethel was a tree, growing off of his shoulder.
Frank Zappa

When we came down from the mountains we were real hillbillies. We didn't even know what Pepsi Cola was.
Butch Stone, manager of Black Oak Arkansas

Some people like to have animals around. I like animals but I thought I'd try a human being because they have more happening.
Grace Slick on her pregnancy

I'd like to publish a political, spiritual and emotional publication or . . . open a restaurant.
Jerry Rubin, 1977

Old friends sat on their park bench like bookends.
Paul Simon

The Blimp, the Blimp! The Mothership!
Captain Beefheart

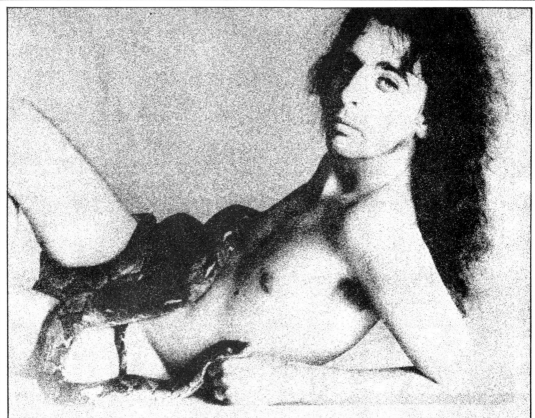

ALICE COOPER

That's not my snake, you know. That snake was much larger than mine. I had to borrow it from a stripper in California when we played there. My snake had the 'flu and kept throwing up her mice.
Alice Cooper

It's just a quiet place to escape the madness, a little English manor house with modern conveniences.
Keith Moon on his 800,000 dollar LA mansion

Who'd want to eat a hamburger? I'm not gonna get into the bullshit to find out what the bull ate.
Captain Beefheart (Don Van Vliet)

We can do what we couldn't do for nine years as the Beatles — we can go out shopping without being recognised.
George Harrison, 1977

A lot of people don't bother about their friends in the vegetable kingdom. They think 'Oh, ah, what can I say? What can a person like myself say to a vegetable . . .?'
Frank Zappa

Life, man, is a gas.
Lou Rawls

The glitter people know where I'm at, the gay people know where I'm at. I make up songs for them. I was doing that in '66 except people were a lot more uptight then. Then you've got the straight people who were Velvet fans. And it's just like a big party.
Lou Reed

In man's evolution he has created the cities and motor traffic rumble, but give me half a chance and I'd be taking off my clothes and living in the jungle.
Ray Davies

I went aaarrrggghhh on the drums, broke the bass drum pedal, and two skins and got off. I figured that was it.
Keith Moon's audition for the High Numbers

People would tell us it was violent, it was grotesque, it was perverted. We said: What are you talking about? It's fun.
Lou Reed, on Warhol's Exploding Plastic Inevitable, 1966

It takes a lot to laugh, it takes a train to cry.
Bob Dylan

WE SHALL OVERCOME

Politics is nothing more than the search of certain individuals for private power.
Jim Morrison

The underground is a bunch of cats who can't pay their bills.
Anonymous

Everywhere I hear the sound of marching, charging feet, boy 'cos summer's here and the time is right for fighting in the street boy. But what can a poor boy do, except to sing in a rock 'n' roll band?
Mick Jagger and Keith Richard

I'm a Citizens for Boysenberry Jam fan.
Paul Simon

The youth revolution in America is a hype. I like Agnew, but I don't like that Nixon.
Joe MacDonald

Suppose they gave a war and no-one came?
Arlo Guthrie

You might wake up in the morning and find your poor selves dead.
Mick Jagger and Keith Richard

I've seen life and I think I know who's controlling the world. And after what I've seen of the state of this world, I've never been so damned scared in all my life.
David Bowie

Don't follow leaders. Watch the parkin' meters.
Bob Dylan

Be the first one on your block to have your boy come home in a box.
Joe MacDonald

The pump don't work, 'cause the vandals took the handles.
Bob Dylan

The old get old, the young get younger, they got the guns but we got the numbers.
Jim Morrison

Some men rob you with a six-gun, others rob you with a fountain pen.
Woody Guthrie

Who Are The Brain Police?
Frank Zappa

The police in New York City chased a boy right through the park and in a case of mistaken identity they put a bullet through his heart.
Mick Jagger and Keith Richard

For the countless confused, accused, misused, strung-out ones an' worse. An' for every hung-up person in the whole wide universe.
Bob Dylan

DAVID BOWIE/PHOTO BY SHEILA ROCK

LEONARD COHEN

There can be no free men unless there are free women.
Leonard Cohen

The playboys and playgirls ain't a-gonna own my world.
Bob Dylan

Nobody likes a stubborn, independent woman. I'm not shaking my ass to be famous.
Bonnie Raitt

Woman Is The Nigger Of The World
John Lennon and Yoko Ono

You don't need a weatherman to know which way the wind blows.
Bob Dylan

Wednesday I watched the riot. I seen the cops out on the street. I watched them throwin' rocks and stuff and chokin' in the heat.
Frank Zappa

I'm not going to be fucked around by men in suits sitting on their fat arses in the city.
John Lennon, during the Beatles break-up

Kick Out The James, Motherfuckers!
The MC5

Gimme an F . . . gimme a U . . . gimme a C . . . gimme a K!!
Country Joe and the Fish

I can't say 'fuck' on a record. Fuck is a nice word. Fuck means something pretty, I like fuck. And I can't say it on record
David Crosby

DAVID CROSBY

I've always felt alienated from the Woodstock Generation, felt out of psychedelia, because, like most pop musicians, I was into it before the masses and when it became big I was extremely ill.
Pete Townshend

You have proven something to the world — that half a million kids can get together for fun and music and have nothing but fun and music.
Max Yasgur, owner of the grounds which held the Woodstock Festival

'Woodstock' is a semi-sales job on behalf of the kids.
Mike Wadleigh, maker of the 'Woodstock' movie

You've all been beautiful, even those of you who tore down the fences.
Announcement at the Isle of Wight Festival, 1970

We represent the only true patriotism left.
Frank Zappa

I went up there, I said 'Shrink, I wanna kill! I wanna kill!! I wanna see blood and gore and guts and veins in my teeth. Eat dead, burnt bodies! I mean — kill. Kill!!'
Arlo Guthrie

There's some little jerk in the FBI getting papers on me six feet high.
Mick Jagger and Keith Richard

If one has strong political beliefs, one should do whatever they think is right about them.
Paul Simon

In the last year or six months, Lenny Bruce had a nail tied to his foot and was going around in circles.
Phil Spector

It is only a matter of time before the change maker learns that he is very much alone, perhaps not in his desires, but in his efforts.
Joe McDonald

Those who will not dance will have to be shot.
Tuli Kupferberg, The Fugs

It can't happen here is number one on the list of famous last words.
David Crosby

I laugh at them. I laugh at those parlour-pink revolutionary kids going around saying 'I am a revolutionary by trade'. Bull-fucking pukie — they haven't any idea what it is, man.
David Crosby

If this is the revolution, why are the drinks so fucking expensive?
Graffiti on London's (defunct) 'Revolution' club

JOAN BAEZ/PHOTO BY S.K.R.

We have been trained to be impotent.
Joan Baez

The 1967 bust kind of said — from now on it's heavy. Up 'till then it had been showbiz. Then you knew they considered you outside. They decide who lives outside the law. You're just living.
Keith Richard

We are all outlaws in the eyes of America.
Jefferson Airplane

Oh, but you who philosophize disgrace and criticize all fears, bury the rag deep in your face, for now's the time for your fears.
Bob Dylan

BOB MARLEY

The Devil always come in between politicians and they start quarrelling. Y'have to imagine what really go on, because power become a pride business instead of we live together and trade together and stop the war . . .
Bob Marley

But if you go carrying pictures of Chairman Mao. You ain't gonna make it with anyone anyhow.
John Lennon and Paul McCartney

We were discriminated against all the time. If we were coloured, we'd really be able to kick up a stink about it. I'm not, so I have to put up with it. Everyone with long hair does.
Jimmy Page

Deep in my heart I do believe that we shall overcome some day.
Pete Seeger

All your property is target for your enemy, and your enemy is . . . we.
Paul Kantner

I shall now proceed to entangle the entire area.
David Crosby

We have fun, the kids have fun, the cops have fun. It's kind of a weird triangle.
Jim Morrison

Subversive? Of course we're subversive. But if they really believe that you can start a revolution with a record, they're wrong. I wish we could. We're more subversive at live appearances.
Keith Richard, 1969

Me and my gal, my gal's son. We got met with a tear gas bomb, I don't even know why we came.
Bob Dylan

The BBC is a great quivering mess creeping into the 1940s out of the 1920s.
John Peel, 1967

Anyone who is disturbed by the idea of newts in a nightclub is potentially dangerous.
Frank Zappa

I don't think politics is a workable system any more, I think they gotta invent something better.
David Crosby

It's a bit difficult to get hippies organised into anything.
Grace Slick

I don't need the kind of law and order that tends to keep a good man underground.
Gram Parsons

San Quentin may you rot and burn in hell!
Johnny Cash

Cancel my subscription to the resurrection. Send my credentials to the house of detention.
The Doors

It increases my paranoia, like looking in my mirror and seeing a police car.
David Crosby

So come out Lyndon with your hands held high. Drop your guns, baby, and reach for the sky.
Joe MacDonald

I'm going to run for President and when I get elected I'll assassinate myself — that'll set a precedent.
Spencer Dryden, Jefferson Airplane

You should have the luck of the Irish, and wish you was English instead.
John Lennon and Yoko Ono

I've always been attracted to ideas that were about revolt against authority. When you make your peace with authority you become authority.
Jim Morrison

You smash it — I'll build around it.
John Lennon

Take a day and walk around, watch the Nazis run your town.
Frank Zappa

War's good business, so give your son and I'd rather have my country die for me.
Grace Slick

We piss anywhere, man.
The Rolling Stones, 1965

The first duty of a revolutionary is to get away with it.
Abbie Hoffman

The Revolution is gonna be won under the influence of Ripple and Red Mountain wine.
Brother Jesse Crawford, White Panther Party

WE SHALL OVERCOME

We're tired of jerking off — we want to start fucking again.
Jerry Garcia

The Indian's never going to get a damn thing 'till he goes out and scalps a few people. Then he'll get attention.
Ray Charles

The whole earth is in jail, and we're plotting this incredible jailbreak.
Wavy Gravy

The truth about America is sick, and I tell it.
Swamp Dogg

To shoot a robot genocidal policeman in the defence of life is a sacred act.
Timothy Leary

A high energy culture prepares you for the revolution, equals constant high energy change. It's the difference between eating something and turning it into shit against turning it into energy to build things with.
John Sinclair

Every revolutionary needs a colour TV.
Jerry Rubin

Power is a politician, but they are so full of corruption. They're the ones who get across to everyone.
Mick Jones, The Clash

The intellectuals would be better off if they wrote their programme on the tits of naked women.
Jerry Rubin, 1967

Everybody has to find his own way to be free.
Bob Dylan

It's more important to be dissatisfied. I should think people crave any alternative to Margaret Thatcher.
Richard Thompson

'Protest' is not my word. I've never thought of myself as such. The word 'protest', I think, was made up for people undergoing surgery . . . a normal person in his righteous mind would have to have hiccups to pronounce it properly.
Bob Dylan

SWAMP DOG

SEX WITH STARS

If he doesn't strum a guitar and sing like a sex maniac, he's nobody.
Anonymous groupie's dictum

If you can't get cunt you want to be a rock 'n' roll something so you can get it. And when you have it, you throw it out on the street. Then you get better versions of it.
Kim Fowley, producer

I'm 24 years old and beautiful . . . pink hanging down my legs, sequins all around my bottom and pearls hanging round my neck. I'm the bronze Liberace.
Little Richard

With this group, the roadies get all the chicks.
The James Gang

Suzy Creamcheese, oh baby what's got into you?
Frank Zappa

In all the time I was on the road I must have laid a million girls, a few boys and the odd goat. The goats were alright, too, only you had to go 'round the other end to kiss them.
Ronnie Hawkins

On stage I make love to 25,000 different people, then I go home alone.
Janis Joplin

I love to hear boys shouting for me, just like I shouted for the Stones.
Patti Smith

Bet your mama don't know you can scratch like that. I bet she never saw you scratch my back.
Mick Jagger and Keith Richard

GREGG ALLMAN

I'm choosy, I was a virgin until I was twenty.
Gregg Allman

Hello, I love you, won't you tell me your name?
The Doors

As long as Christ knew I wasn't a sissy, I had nothing to fear.
Tiny Tim

I want every drumhead in my set to be painted with the face of the first girl who gave me the crabs.
Frank Beard, ZZ Top

JOHNNY WINTER

I want a guitar that's smart enough to play all my licks so I could concentrate on acting like Mick Jagger for the girls in the audience. But it would have to be dumb enough not to go after the girls itself.
Johnny Winter

You look for certain things in certain towns. Chicago, for instance, is notorious for sort of two things at once. Balling two chicks, or three, in combination acts.
Jimmy Page

I haven't seen her in two years . . . In the old days. Beautiful. Used to wipe herself with the American flag after doin' it. And the way she dropped acid lying on old Fats Domino records.
Bob Dylan on Joan Baez, 1969

You get to ball the prettiest boys, smoke the best dope and meet all the most far-out people.
Pattie Cakes in the film 'Groupies'

Fucking groupies, I'm telling you, the next one that pushes herself at me, I'm gonna piss all over her, just piss all over her.
John Osborne, Black Sabbath

I'm saving the bass player for Omaha.
Janis Joplin

We're the world's ugliest band. When we play I expect to find puke in the aisles.
Bobby Colombey, Blood Sweat and Tears

I've lived for years with people saying I'm a poof but I don't give a damn. My best friends know me and that's all that matters. Even before I became a Christian I wasn't going to lay loads of chicks to prove myself. I'm about the only one around who hasn't had a nervous breakdown.
Cliff Richard

I'm not too hung up on the beauty stakes. I have an eye for all the customers.
Rod Stewart

Women think I'm tasty but they're always trying to waste me. Make me burn the candle right down.
Mick Jagger and Keith Richard

I feel sexless on stage, I'm neither man nor woman. A lot of people think I'm terribly butch.
Marsha Hunt

Very rare that chicks hit on me. I think they're afraid of me.
Frank Zappa

You were at school and you were pimply and no-one wanted to know you. You get into a group and you've got thousands of chicks there. And there you are with thousands of little girls screaming their heads off. Man, it's *power* . . . phew!
Eric Clapton

Roland the Roadie loves Gertrude the Groupie and Gertrude the Groupie loves groups.
Shel Silverstein

Put on the Dead and spread.
'Rolling Stone' magazine record review of 'Live Dead', 1969

Maybe if the audience can see a cock through a pair of trousers, that must make you a sex symbol.
Robert Plant

People are really surprised when they meet us and find out that we're all straight.
Alice Cooper

ALICE COOPER

BONNIE RAITT

I don't want to see any faces at this party I haven't sat on.
Bonnie Raitt

You know, the Beatles' tours were like Fellini's 'Satyricon'. I mean we had that image, but man our tours were like something else. When we hit town, we hit it. We were not pissing around.
John Lennon

I only remember a city by its chicks.
Jimi Hendrix

Give me a couple of drinks, and I'll be the bitch.
Elton John

Honey I miss your two-toned kisses, legs wrapped around me tight. If I ever get back to Fun City girl I'm gonna make ya scream all night.
Mick Jagger and Keith Richard

Well she was just seventeen. You know what I mean.
John Lennon and Paul McCartney

You've got to teach that pussy how to whistle.
Sunnyland Slim

I think about fucking a lot when I play my guitar.
Lita Ford, the Runaways

Levon Helm had more meat than the Toronto abbatoirs.
Ronnie Hawkins

Boy, wouldn't thirty million women like to be where I am now.
Priscilla Presley, when lying on a beach between Elvis and Tom Jones

Uh-oh, I think I exposed myself out there.
Jim Morrison

I hate when Grace does that sexy shit on stage. Man, it really makes me want to puke. She reminds me of my mother — she's *not* sexy.
Marty Balin

We're not opposed to stage flash — we just don't want to look like a bunch of faggots.
J. Geils Band

Playboy's like Doris Day, in the nude. I'm sure if I stripped off Doris Day's bra, I'd find another bra underneath.
Jimmy Page

He sure left his mark, that cat. I know of five kids, at least. All by different chicks and they all look like Brian.
Keith Richard on Brian Jones

We had parties that Nero would have been ashamed to attend.
Ronnie Hawkins

The offers to fill my bed would keep it full for a fortnight.
Jimmy Page

Girls from all over the world love to write my name on the toilet walls at the Whiskey A Go Go.
Frank Zappa

She was common, flirty, she looked about thirty. I would have run away but I was on my own. She told me later she's a machine operator. She said she liked the way I held the microphone.
Mick Jagger and Keith Richard

I wouldn't let Grace Slick blow me.
Marty Balin

There's really no reason to have women on a tour unless they've got a job to do. The only other reason is to screw. Otherwise they get bored. They just sit around and moan.
Mick Jagger

It's Rene, the docker's delight. She lets the ships in every night.
Small Faces

Print a famous foreskin and world will beat a path to your door.
Jann Wenner, editor 'Rolling Stone' magazine

Mick is so exciting yet at the same time peaceful to be with. We don't have to go anywhere exotic to enjoy life. As a matter of fact our most pleasant dates have been spent picknicking in his back garden.
Patti d'Arbanville

You don't wanna see my trousers fall down, now, do you?
Mick Jagger

Uh-oh, me trousers is falling . . . I told you we wanted to give you something special tonight.
Rod Stewart

We steer completely clear of anything suggestive. We take a lot of care with lyrics because we don't want to offend anybody. The music is the main thing and it's just as easy to write acceptable words.
Bill Haley, 1954

Then in comes his daughter whose name was Rita. She looked like she stepped out of La Dolce Vita.
Bob Dylan

It's a life with a lot of pain, being a groupie. People just leave you, always leaving you, leaving you.
Sally, a groupie

I think Mick Jagger would be astounded and amazed if he realized to how many people he is not a sex symbol.
Angie Bowie

I can see that you're fifteen years old. No I don't want your ID.
Mick Jagger and Keith Richard

What say we hop in the trunk of your Gremlin and get our rocks off!
Frank Zappa

Women should be obscene and not heard.
John Lennon

Freud would have a heyday with me.
David Bowie

Fuck Grace Slick? I never even kissed her. And it's the smartest, best damn thing I ever done.
Marty Balin

Hallelujah! Someone's feeling my balls.
Steve Marriott

MARIA MULDAUR

I want to be a singer long after I'm not so hot to look at.
Maria Muldaur

I've got to get this make-up off now. People think I go walking round in it.
Roy Wood, Wizzard

I want a cunt transplant in the back of my guitar so I could fuck it while I'm playing.
Punky Meadows, AC/DC

Luther (Grosvenor) is such a jerk. He's such an easy fuck and he thinks he's so cool.
Brenda and Diana in the film 'Groupies'

I haven't met anybody I'd like to settle down with — of either sex.
Elton John

Robin Tyner's so fucking sensuous that he made a friend of mine come in her pants. *That's getting down!!* The most pleasing part of Rob's anatomy is his legs — as the Five's music builds to a crescendo, so every muscle in Rob's legs tightens and pulsates like a fucking cock! Fred 'Sonic' 'Mad-dog' Smith is so far out. He fucks his guitar and you're writhing with ecstasy, begging for more . . .'
Part of a Press Release from Translove Energies for the MC5, 1969

None of us rock 'n' rollers could understand all that fuss about Jerry Lee Lewis marrying a thirteen year old. All us Southern cats knew she was only twelve.
Ronnie Hawkins

MICK JAGGER

By the time it was over he had lapped and nuzzled his guitar with his lips and tongue, caressed it with his inner thighs, jabbed at it with a series of powerful pelvis thrusts. Even the little girls who'd come to see the Monkees understood what this was about.
Jimi Hendrix at Monterey Pop, 1967 by Lillian Roxon

My whole act is made up from different girls I've been with. I took the walk from a girl in Hollywood, the body movements from a dancer in the Ed Sullivan show and the pout from Chrissie Shrimpton. Now I see on TV that Tom Jones is copying the pouting bit. But I don't think it will work with him, because when he pouts it looks like a bassett hound.
P. J. Proby

When we started filming I could feel George looking at me and I was a bit embarrassed. Then when he was giving me his autograph he put seven kisses under his name. I thought he must like me a little.
Patti Harrison, nee Boyd, on meeting her future husband while playing a schoolgirl in 'Hard Day's Night'

Sometimes an orgasm is better than being on stage. Sometimes being on stage is better than an orgasm.
Mick Jagger

There stood Rita, lookin' just like Tony Perkins.
Bob Dylan

So we had an affair. You must be pretty bad, I don't even remember you.
Bianca Jagger to Warren Beatty, after he had told Hollywood gossip writers of their alleged affair.

The idea of sex with a man doesn't turn me off, but I don't express it. I satisfied my curiosity about that fifteen years ago . . . strange experiences with older boys. But men don't particularly turn me on.
Daryl Hall

But I'm not tired.
Attributed to Gilbert O'Sullivan when invited to bed by 'The Happy Hooker', Xaviera Hollander

As far as I'm concerned the benefit of being a black Irishman is that I pull more chicks.
Phil Lynott, Thin Lizzy

Young . . . Tender . . . Old . . . Don't make no difference — dem girls.
Junior Wells

Rock is cock.
John Hallowell

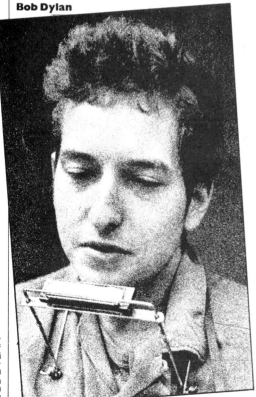

BOB DYLAN

THE LOOK OF LOVE

I know it's not much but it's the best I can do. My gift is my song and this one's for you.
Bernie Taupin

I wish they all could be California girls.
Brian Wilson

I think music should make people sit back and want to touch each other.
Jim Croce

It must be love, it's a bitch.
Mick Jagger and Keith Richard

Holy smoke, a-land sakes alive, I never thought this could happen to me.
Aaron Shroeder and David Hill

Because you're mine, I walk the line
Johnny Cash

To know, know, know you is to love, love, love you.
Phil Spector

I gave her my heart but she wanted my soul but don't think twice, it's alright.
Bob Dylan

You may be plain, but you're pretty in the morning.
Randy Newman

And in the end the love you take is equal to the love you make.
John Lennon and Paul McCartney

Be-bop-a-lula she's my baby, Be-bop-a-lula I don't mean maybe.
Gene Vincent and Sheriff Tex Davis

Went to a dance lookin' for romance, saw Barbara Ann so I thought I'd take a chance.
Fred Fasert

Tell me a story about how you adore me.
Mick Jagger and Keith Richard

All I really want to do is, baby, be friends with you.
Bob Dylan

Yeah, when you call my name, Salivate like a Pavlov dog.
Mick Jagger and Keith Richard

None of the guys go steady 'cos it wouldn't be right to leave your best girl home on a Saturday night.
Brian Wilson

JAMES TAYLOR

She's a piece of ass. It bothers me. If she looks at another man, I'll kill her.
James Taylor

Sometimes I wish, often I wish. I never knew some of those secrets of yours.
Carly Simon

I once had a girl, or should I say she once had me.
John Lennon and Paul McCartney

Her name was Wanda and I don't mind admitting I was scared to death. Finally I got up enough nerve to give her a peck on the cheek. And she shrieked 'Pat Boone, you kiss like a cow!'
Pat Boone's first kiss, recalled in 1959

Love is what you feel for a dog or a pussy cat, it doesn't apply to humans and if it does it just shows how low you are. It shows your intelligence isn't clicking.
Johnny Rotten, Sex Pistols

I lived with someone once for two years. But I decided that to be married you had to make married music. And I'm not ready for that.
Bruce Springsteen

Though my wife still respects me, I really abuse her. I am having an affair with a random computer.
Mick Jagger and Keith Richard

Domesticity is death.
Mick Jagger

I don't mind other guys dancing with my girl, I don't mind 'cos I know them all pretty well. But I know sometimes I must get out in the light, better leave her behind with the kids, they're alright.
Pete Townshend

My love don't give me presents, I know that she's no peasant.
John Lennon and Paul McCartney

Everybody's got half of a couple
Peter Allen and Carol Sager

Michelle, ma belle, sont les mots qui vont très bien ensemble.
John Lennon and Paul McCartney

You'll never get to heaven if you break my heart, so be very careful not to let us part.
Hal David and Burt Bacharach

Return to sender, address unknown. No such number, no such zone.
Otis Blackwell and Winfield Scott

Woman don't try to love me, don't try to understand. A life upon the road, is the life of an outlaw man.
David Blue

If you gotta go, go now. Or else you gotta stay all night.
Bob Dylan

I'm hungry for learnin', won't you answer me please. Can a man and a woman live together in peace?
Paul Simon

When you say she's looking good, she acts as if it's understood.
John Lennon and Paul McCartney

Go to a show you hope she goes.
John Lennon and Paul McCartney

She's got a ticket to ride, but she don't care.
John Lennon and Paul McCartney

Saw you early this morning with your brand new boy and your Cadillac.
Van Morrison

I'm just looking for an angel with a broken wing — one who couldn't fly away.
Jimmy Page

I'm Left, You're Right, She's Gone.
Song Title

THE LOOK OF LOVE

Intellectually, of course, we didn't believe in getting married. But one doesn't love someone intellectually.
John Lennon

I'm looking for me, you're looking for you. We're looking at each other and we don't know what to do.
Peter Townshend

Well you were easy to fool. When you were in school but you grown up all wrong.
Mick Jagger and Keith Richard

If you really want to be my friend, give me the look of love not jealousy.
Mick Jagger and Keith Richard

She's a twentieth century fox. No tears, no fears, no ruined years, no clocks.
Jim Morrison

There must be fifty ways to leave your lover.
Paul Simon

My girl-friend's gone off with my car and gone back to her Ma and Pa. Telling tales of drunken-ness and cruelty.
Ray Davies

She's got everything she needs, she's an artist, she don't look back.
Bob Dylan

Oh dear, what can I do, baby's in black and I'm feeling blue.
John Lennon and Paul McCartney

She called him Speedoo, but his Christian name was really Mr. Earl.
Paul Simon

We're just a habit like saccharine.
Paul Simon

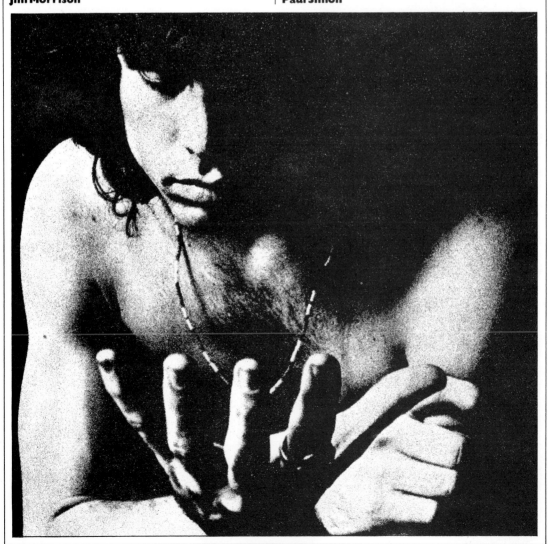

JIM MORRISON

TINY TIM

I was so moved that I shed a tear and put it in an envelope that I always keep in my ukelele.
Tiny Tim, on the occasion of announcing his engagement to Miss Vicki.

Listen honey, you can't put your love out on the street, no, no, no . . . you've got to put your love in a pot, honey, and take it on home.
Janis Joplin.

Don't threaten me with love, baby, let's just go walking in the rain.
Billie Holiday

You can't blame John for falling in love with Yoko any more than you can blame me for falling in love with Linda. At the beginning I was annoyed with him, jealous because of Yoko and afraid about the break-up of a great musical partnership. It took me a year to realise they were in love.
Paul McCartney

I always suspected we would marry one day. I was already playing in an amateur group and on our first date, Alison carried my amplifier.
John Entwhistle, commenting on his marriage in 1967

People think love is an emotion. Love is good sense.
Ken Kesey

Time to face the dawning grey of another lonely day and it's so hard living without you.
Randy Newman

That I let you get so close to me is really no surprise. It'll be lonesome without you but I'll survive.
Joe MacDonald

A lover for your life and nothing more.
Bob Dylan

And the love that loves the love that loves the love that loves the love that loves to love the love that loves to love the love that loves.
Van Morrison

If you try acting sad, you'll only make me glad.
Mick Jagger and Keith Richard

Why, tell me why, did you not treat me right. Love has a nasty habit of disappearing over night.
John Lennon and Paul McCartney

Who wants yesterday's papers. Who wants yesterday's girl?
Mick Jagger and Keith Richard

Everybody's been burned before, everybody knows the pain.
David Crosby

I wanna hold your hand.
John Lennon and Paul McCartney

GENIUS IS PAIN

Godammit! He beat me to it.
Janis Joplin on the death of Jimi Hendrix, 1970

Sometimes I wonder if we don't take ourselves too seriously.
Don Henley, The Eagles

You don't have much part in what you're doing. You're like a trolley-car, shooting down the tracks and you get the electricity from the wire above you and the tracks below.
Roger McGuinn

If I can't give people the best, I'd rather not appear at all.
Elvis Presley

I don't want to be a clown any more. I don't want to be a rock 'n' roll star.
Jimi Hendrix

When I was about twelve I used to think I must be a genius, but nobody's noticed. I used to think whether I'm a genius or I'm mad, which is it? I used to think, well, I can't be mad because nobody's put me away; therefore I'm a genius . . . If there is such a thing as genius, I am one, y'know . . . and if there isn't, I don't care.
John Lennon

I am an artist and should be exempt from shit.
P. J. Proby (James Marcus Smith)

My name is no big deal. It's meaningless. I tried to get rid of the burden of the Bob Dylan myth for a long time.
Bob Dylan

We're definitely outsiders. The Grateful Dead is like *fear*, man.
Jerry Garcia

GENIUS IS PAIN

I'm sick of being Gulliver . . . I just want to go home to Beckenham and watch the telly.
David Bowie after his 1974 Tour

I don't want to be the world's oldest living folk singer.
Joan Baez

I just do my best. I don't say nothing about nobody. Except me. Stay in my place. Speak when spoken to. That's just about it.
Howlin' Wolf (Chester Burnett)

I was going on stage with a band that was a burn. It was like going out and selling parsley on the street and having to meet the people next day. Byrdshit! It wasn't the Byrds — it was the fucking canaries!
David Crosby

Fame threw me for a loop at first. I learned how to swim with it and turn it around. So you can just throw it in the closet and pick it up when you need it.
Bob Dylan

I get tired of singing to the guys I beat up in motion pictures.
Elvis Presley

ELVIS PRESLEY

No-one wants to have a twit image.
Melanie (Safka Schekeryk)

The thing is, I'm not an entertainer. I'm an artist, a musician . . . and there's a great difference.
Van Morrison

I'm like a woman because I have my periods. Every once in a while I get the cramps and do something far-out.
Captain Beefheart (Don Van Vliet)

Brian Wilson never asked for any trouble. He just wrote songs about cars and the beach and everybody nailed the motherfucker to the wall. They really nailed him. That poor motherfucker.
Terry Melcher.

We make a special art in an environment hostile to dreamers.
Frank Zappa

I'd rather retain the position of being a photostat machine with an image, because I think most songwriters are anyway.
David Bowie

I'm just gonna keep on rockin', 'cos if I start saving up bits and pieces of me like that, man, there ain't gonna be nothing left for Janis.
Janis Joplin

There are two ways of doing it. Either I change my name back to McCartney and everybody says it's Paul McCartney's brother, or I leave it as McGear and everybody says it's Paul McCartney's brother.
Mike McGear

I don't relate to all this any differently than if I was a clerk. I wouldn't be telling some guy from a magazine what I did when I went home, so why should I in this business.
Van Morrison

Skip's been and gone from places that you will never get to.
Skip James

LINDA RONSTADT

I finally learned how to sing. It's too bad I had to do all my learning in public.
Linda Ronstadt

Ever since I was born, or maybe when I was two years old, somebody punched me in the ear.
Brian Wilson

I operate in the underdog role.
Art Garfunkel

I don't understand why half the world is still cryin' . . . when the other half of the world is cryin' too, man. I can't get it together . . .
Janis Joplin

Most everybody had written me off. Oh yeah, they all acted like they were proud for me when I straightened up. Some of them are still mad about it, though. I didn't go ahead and die so that they'd have a legend to sing about and put me in hillbilly heaven.
Johnny Cash

I'm a freakin' artist, man, not a fucking racehorse.
John Lennon

An entertainer never stops paying his dues.
José Feliciano

I wish I could go insane or die at times, but I'm not allowed.
Marc Bolan

Success is like a shot of heroin. It's up to you to decide whether you want to continue to put the needle in your arm.
Don McLean

I believed it. I thought I was a fucking genius. Oh Christ, it ruined me.
Kris Kristofferson

A lot of people want us to make it, but there's a self-destructive quality in everything we do.
Ray Davies

Imagine taking off your makeup and nobody knows who you are.
Steven Tyler, Aerosmith

All my life I just wanted to be a beatnik, meet all the heavies, get stoned, get laid, have a good time. That's all I ever wanted, except I knew I had a good voice and I could always get a couple of beers off of it. All of a sudden someone threw me in this rock 'n' roll band . . . and I decided then and there that was it. I never wanted to do anything else. It was better than it had been with any man, y'know. Maybe that's the trouble . . .
Janis Joplin

DON EVERLY

The Everly Brothers died ten years ago.
Don Everly at their Farewell Concert, 1973

Christ you know it ain't easy, you know how hard it can be. The way things are going, they're gonna crucify me.
John Lennon

I'm not a genius, I'm just a hard-working guy.
Brian Wilson

Pain is what we're in most of the time. And I think the bigger the pain, the more Gods we need.
John Lennon

I don't do. I am.
P. J. Proby (James Marcus Smith)

More and more, with every song I write, I try to record what I see and leave out what I think.
Tom Paxton

Somebody told me that I don't make small-talk and that's why men hate me.
Yoko Ono

When Joan (Baez) and I sing 'Blowing In The Wind' it's like an old folk song to me. I never *occurs* to me that I'm the person who wrote that.
Bob Dylan

I'm tired of being victimised by people who are dedicated to a snappy phrase.
Linda Ronstadt

I don't sound like nobody.
Elvis Presley

Sometimes I don't feel as if I'm a person at all. I'm just a collection of other people's ideas.
David Bowie

I'm too young to be a legend.
Mick Fleetwood

Basically our situation is on the borderline of collapse all the time anyway.
Jerry Garcia

JERRY GARCIA

Pleasure, I never seek pleasure. There was a time years ago when I sought a lot of pleasure because I'd had a lot of pain. But I found out there was a subtle relationship between pleasure and pain. So now I do what I have to do without looking for pleasure in it.
Bob Dylan

My life has been what you might call an uneventful one, and it seems there is not much of interest to tell . . .
Buddy Holly, writing his autobiography aged 16

Where am I running to? There's no place to go. Just put on my make-up and get me to the show.
Alice Cooper

I know that one day a big artist is going to be killed on stage . . . and I keep thinking it's going to be me.
David Bowie

We're from the Mid-West, we don't know any big words.
Rob Tyner, MC5

I do think it is a bit strange that all we ever talk about is me.
Bianca Jagger

If I had the capabilities of being something other than I am, I would. It's no fun being an artist.
John Lennon

I'm not just a musical *Time* magazine.
Don McLean

I've been put up to be the Big Bad Wolf of rock 'n' roll for a long time.
Captain Beefheart (Don Van Vliet)

The only reason journalists call me a myth or a legend is because they simply can't think of anything else to write.
Van Morrison

I don't want to spend the rest of my life changing my phone-number every thirty days.
Van Morrison

They're not the 'good old days' to me.
Johnny Cash

When I was younger, so much younger than today I never needed anybody's help in any way, but now these days are gone I'm not so self assured . . .
John Lennon and Paul McCartney

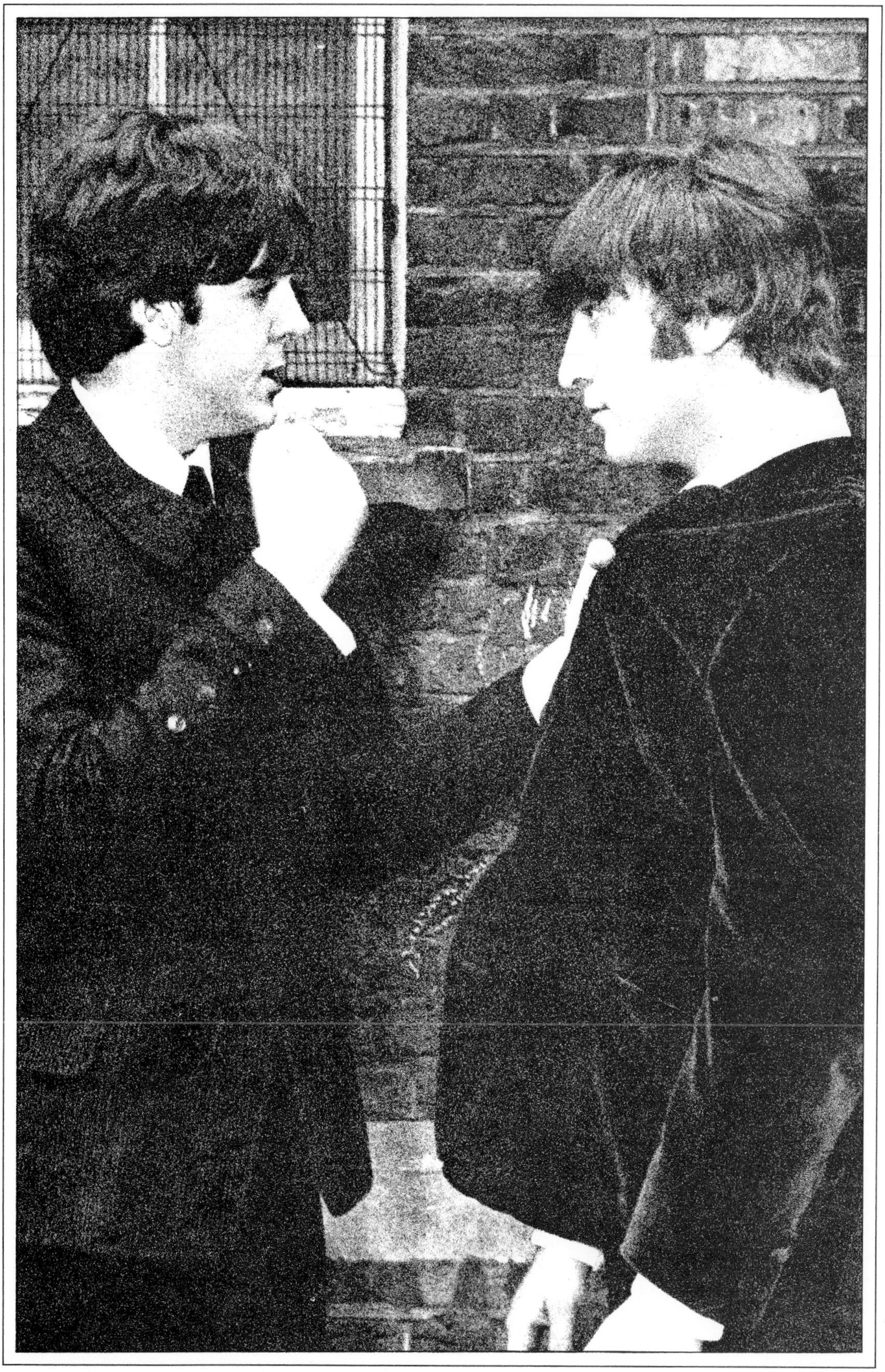

JOHN LENNON & PAUL MCCARTNEY/PHOTO BY LESLIE BRYCE

JONI MITCHELL

PETER FRAMPTON

Inside I'm thinking, you're smiling phoney, you're being a star.
Joni Mitchell

Well I used to fly high but I crashed out the sky.
David Essex

If you don't *know*, man, then there's no pain.
John Lennon

Please don't judge me too harshly.
Brian Jones

If I seem free, it's because I'm always running.
Jimi Hendrix

You can't rely on inspiration every night.
Janis Joplin

Winners got scars too.
Johnny Cash

I feel so suicidal just like Dylan's Mr. Jones.
John Lennon and Paul McCartney

The only thing I have to do with being a genius is that I occasionally wear Levis.
Captain Beefheart (Don Van Vliet)

They're selling post-cards of the hanging. They're painting the passports brown. The beauty parlour is filled with sailors. The circus is in town.
'Desolation Row' by Bob Dylan

Is that what you feel about it? Do you think it's all bullshit?
Peter Frampton

I didn't want to grow up with no-one knowin' me but the neighbourhood people. I wanted the world to know a *lot* about me. I thank my God I got it through . . .
Muddy Waters

Sometimes I can make myself feel better with music, but other times it's still hard to go to sleep at night.
Bob Dylan

Having waited so long to be successful, I found out it was a terrible anti-climax.
Rod Stewart

It's very hard to live up to an image.
Elvis Presley

If I haven't been through what I write about, the songs aren't worth anything.
Bob Dylan

Having a Number One single, being on the cover of *Rolling Stone* and all this other bullshit that's happening — I always thought I would *feel* something, but I just feel numb.
Daryl Hall

I'm warming up to the idea of an asylum.
John Lennon

GROWN UP ALL RIGHT

I had a banana band in high school.
Bob Dylan

I'm just a kid from Hoboken.
Frank Sinatra

All I ever wanted to be was a featured sideman with a famous rock 'n' roll star. I guess that if either Eddie Cochran or Buddy Holly had still been alive I'd have been more concerned with trying to get into their backing group instead of forming my own band.
John Fogerty, Creedence Clearwater Revival

Being born in Scotland carries with it certain responsibilities.
Derek Taylor

And we were the Wild Children back in 1945, when all the soldiers came marching home, love looks, love looks in their eyes, in their eyes.
Van Morrison

I wanted to be a dentist from about Grade 6 . . . then I heard some R&B and it kinda changed my life.
Roy Kenner, James Gang

JOHN FOGERTY/PHOTO BY BRIAN MOODY

FRANK ZAPPA

Everyone in town knows I'm a handsome football star. I sing and dance and spray my hair and drive a shiny car.
Frank Zappa

I first realized I could sing at two years of age. I was eight years old and they entered me in a talent competition. I wore glasses, no music and I won. I got a whipping the same day, my mother whipped me for something. Destroyed my ego completely.
Elvis Presley

Your teeth are clean, but your mind is capped.
John Lennon

My father knew a lot of guitar players and most of them didn't work. So I'd better make up my mind whether I wanted to be a guitar player or an electrician, because he never knew a guitar player who was worth a damn.
Elvis Presley

After reading Tolkien, I just had to have a place in the country.
Robert Plant

What's good enough for San Francisco is good enough for the world.
Jann Wenner, editor, 'Rolling Stone' Magazine

I like punk . . . things have changed, but the things that made me angry as a kid make me angry now.
Roger Daltrey

If you're a mod, you're a mod twenty-four hours a day. Even working with other people you're still a mod.
Anonymous Mod in 'Generation X', Tandem Paperbacks

Is there any MP with the courage to introduce a bill compelling boys to have their hair cut?
'Daily Mirror,' November 21st, 1964. Letter from Mrs. K. R. M. of Plymouth

When I was two feet off the ground I collected broken glass and cats. When I was three feet off the ground I made drawings of animals and forest fires. When I was four feet off the ground I discovered boys and bicycles.
Joni Mitchell

I was a little loose in the attic. When I was a kid I tied do-rags around my head tight. I was scared my soul would fly out at night.
Patti Smith

Most of the people I associated with were unsavoury types . . . but to live outside the law you must be honest.
John Kay, Steppenwolf

JOHN KAY/PHOTO BY L.F.I.

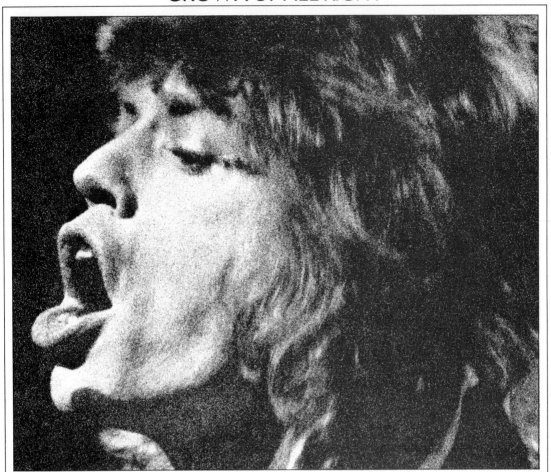

MICK JAGGER

I never was a teenager, I don't remember doing any teenage songs.
Mick Jagger.

Michael could be a very good impersonator if he wants to, he could probably make a living from it.
Mrs. Eva Jagger

I don't know what it is — I just fell into it really. My daddy and I were laughing about it the other day. He looked at me and said 'The last thing I can remember is I was working in a can factory and you were driving a truck'.
Elvis Presley

Kids resent doing things around the house. They resent parents' attitudes. In fact, they resent parents.
Mike Stoller

John played all this stuff and I remember thinking he smelled a bit drunk. Quite a nice chap, but he was still a bit drunk.
Paul McCartney

I am the product of a haphazard musical environment which I suppose makes me a folk artist.
James Taylor

Ah, but I was so much older then, I'm younger than that now.
Bob Dylan

They started to raise me in Mississippi, but the rope broke.
Gus Cannon, harp player

I think I had one voice lesson. The teacher told me not to take any more because it might affect my delivery.
Johnny Cash

The Beach Boys had everyone in England surfing. Blokes were bleaching their hair blonde and carrying surf boards through Soho.
Terry Melcher

Frankly, I still want to play as if I were a child.
Captain Beefheart (Don Van Vliet)

KEITH RICHARD/PHOTO BY GERED MANKOWITZ

So I get on this fucking train one morning and there's Jagger and under his arm he has four or five albums. I haven't seen him since the time I bought an ice-cream off him and we haven't hung around together since we were five, six, ten years old. We recognized each other straight off . . . and under his arm he's got Chuck Berry and Little Walter, Muddy Waters . . .
Keith Richard reminisces on his meeting Mick Jagger for keeps

Hibbing's a good ol' town, I ran away from it when I was 10, 12, 13, 15, 15½, 17 an' 18. I been caught an' brought back all but once.
Bob Dylan

I used to see them drivers with their shirts off, handkerchiefs around their neck, a little cap on their head. They looked daring to me. I always dreamed of being a real wild truck-driver.
Elvis Presley

More than a teen-age, jean-age idol now! Even if you wear clerical grey to match your hair, you'll thrill to Elvis Presley — he's a revelation as the convict climbing from shame to fame, song by song.
Ad copy for 'Jailhouse Rock' movie

The word is not 'international phenomenon', the word is 'parental nightmare'.
Bob Dylan on Rock 'n' Roll

Knowing, perhaps, that the ruse couldn't last, the Beatles have hinted at the truth in every successive album. On the 'Sgt. Pepper' album centrefold, only Paul faces away from the camera . . . on the 'Magical Mystery Tour' insert, only Paul wears a black rose . . . 'Revolution No. 9' on the double album contains the phrase 'I buried Paul' when played backwards . . . 'Abbey Road' shows the Beatles walking in single file. The first two, John and Ringo, wear mourning clothes, 'Paul' is barefoot and dressed for burial, George follows in the work clothes of an English gravedigger.
'Rat Magazine', October 29th, 1969, launches the 'Paul is dead' hoax.

We all live in a yellow submarine.
John Lennon and Paul McCartney

Itsy Bitsie Teeny Weeny Yellow Polka Dot Bikini.
Paul Vance and Lee Pockriss

I generally play rock music when I perform open heart surgery. It's a long proved observation that the rhythm of music played in the background will set a tempo for work. And it also helps ease tension among the operating team.
Dr. Gerald K. LeMole, Philadelphia, 1971

My past is so complicated you wouldn't believe it.
Bob Dylan, 1965

How many roads must a man walk down, before you call him a man?
Bob Dylan

When I'm watching my TV and that man comes on to tell me how white my shirts can be. Well he can't be a man, 'cos he doesn't smoke the same cigarettes as me.
Mick Jagger and Keith Richard

Like a bridge over troubled water I will ease your mind.
Paul Simon

It's alright as long as he doesn't smoke or drink alcohol. I know all about his girl-friends.
Mrs. Simmons, mother of Kiss's Gene Simmons

Twenty years of schoolin' and they put you on the day shift.
Bob Dylan

When I was nine I went to a boarding school and on the first day I was surrounded and taken to a bathroom where I was confronted by a bath of used toilet paper. I had to either get in or get beaten up. I got beaten up.
Joe Strummer, The Clash

We were twelve then, but in spite of his sideboards we went on to become teenage pals.
Paul McCartney on meeting John Lennon in 1955

Many people ask what are the Beatles? Why the Beatles? Ugh, Beatles? How did the name arrive? So we will tell you. It came in a vision: a man appeared on a flaming pie and said unto them 'From now on you are Beatles with an A'. 'Thank you, Mister Man', they said, thanking him. And so they were Beatles.
John Lennon

Mars ain't the kind of place to raise your kids. In fact it's cold as hell and there's no-one there to raise them if you did.
Bernie Taupin

Because of the artificial popularity that they (the music press) have created out of punk rock, they have broken the backs of young people for the next two or three years who really have got some genuine artistry to offer. They will have the label 'punk' stuck on them no matter what they do.
Ian Anderson, Jethro Tull

The copper came to the door to tell us about the accident. It was just like it's supposed to be, the way it is in the films. Asking if I were her son and all that. Then he told us and we both went white. It was the worst thing that ever happened to me.
John Lennon on his mother's death in a road accident in 1958

Welcome to my life tattoo, we've a long time together, me and you.
Pete Townshend

I began singing at 16. I wasn't in school, I was just goofin'. I've always been singing along with records, my Dad was a disc jockey and it's been what I wanted to do.
Ron 'Pigpen' McKernan

DAVID BOWIE/PHOTO BY BYRON NEWMAN

My basic outlook is still much the same as it was when I was 14.
David Bowie

My dad was very strict and taught me I must always respect my elders. I couldn't speak unless I was spoken to first by grown-ups. So I've always been very quiet.
Jimi Hendrix

His pompadour was high and his hip action was wicked when Elvis was still a pimply kid mowing lawns in Memphis.
Little Richard, described by Lillian Roxon

The killer awoke before dawn. He put his boots on. He took a face from the ancient gallery and he walked on down the hall.
Jim Morrison

For most people the fantasy is driving around in a big car, having all the chicks you want and being able to pay for it. It always has been, still is, and always will be. And anyone who says it isn't is talking bullshit.
Mick Jagger

My Uncle Used To Love Me But She Died.
Roger Miller

And though she feels she is in a play, she is anyway.
John Lennon and Paul McCartney

In this one — 'Revolution' — of course, the Beatles are simply telling the Maoists that Fabian gradualism is working and that the Maoists might blow it by getting the public excited before they are ready for 'Revolution'. The song makes it perfectly clear that the Beatles are on the side of, and working for 'Revolution' and that their war is going to be successful — 'it's gonna be alright'. In short, 'Revolution' takes the Moscow line against the Trotskyites and the Progressive Labour Party, based on Lenin's 'Leftwing Extremism, An Infantile Disorder'.
Gary Allen, 'That Music'

You'd better stop, look around, here it comes, here comes your nineteenth nervous breakdown.
Mick Jagger and Keith Richard

BLOWING IN THE MIND

It's a funny thing about marijuana — when you first begin smoking it you see things in a soothing, easy going new light. All of a sudden the world is stripped of its dirty grey shrouds and becomes one bellyful of giggles.
Mezz Mezzrow

If you claim this drug, LSD, is going to make a man a saint, a yogi, which needs months, years, a lifetime, you can better, more profitably, make a simpler drug, one that makes a man a doctor or a lawyer.
Swami Satchidananda

Grass, it sits you down on your fanny — you can't do anything but see things.
Joni Mitchell

I've taken LSD thirty-eight times. The reason I keep taking it is to get over my compulsion for counting the trips.
Paul Krassner

Some say live by the gun die by the gun — others say let's get high.
San Francisco 'Oracle'

Macrobiotic hippies — nothing fascinates them more than dealing with meat.
Ken Kesey

I declare that the Beatles are mutants. Prototypes of evolutionary agents endowed with a mysterious power to create a new human species — a young race of laughing freemen.
Timothy Leary

Nothing is real and nothing to get hung about.
John Lennon and Paul McCartney

Out here on the perimeter, there are no stars. Out here we is stoned, immaculate.
The Doors

Crazy Miranda, she lives off propaganda. She believes in anything she reads.
Grace Slick

Everything I say will come out just a little bit different. I don't mean on the transcript, but as it leaves my mind and comes through my mouth, it gets a little bit messed up just around my mouth where the words start . . . doing it.
Paul McCartney

PAGE 93

BLOWING IN THE MIND

GEORGE HARRISON

I'm a tidy man. I keep my socks in the socks drawer and my stash in the stash box. Anything else they must have brought.
George Harrison on his bust for 120 joints, 1969

She said 'I know what it's like to be dead'.
John Lennon and Paul McCartney

The Magical Mystery Tour
Song Title by John Lennon and Paul McCartney

He blew his mind out in a car. He didn't notice that the lights had changed.
John Lennon and Paul McCartney

I'll stay a week and get the crabs and take a bus back home. I'm really just a phoney, but forgive me 'cos I'm stoned.
Frank Zappa

Show me that I'm everywhere and get me home for tea.
John Lennon and Paul McCartney

Now everybody's seen God and so, big deal, it ain't even cool any more.
Jerry Garcia, 1975

Hey Mr. Tambourine Man play a song for me. In the jingle-jangle morning I'll come followin' you.
Bob Dylan

Hey punk, where you goin' with that flower in your hand? Well I'm going up to Frisco to join a psychedelic band.
Frank Zappa

Somebody once described me as the original hippie, and that's because of the flowery lyrics, you know, and also because of the buzz we give out.
Robert Plant

Turn off your mind, relax, and float down stream.
John Lennon and Paul McCartney

Pop music is just hard work, long hours, and a lot of drugs.
Mama Cass Elliott

I'd love to turn you on.
John Lennon and Paul McCartney

The Beatles misused that responsibility and turned a whole generation onto drugs. We're going to be very careful about how we use our new fame.
Daryl Dragon, 'Captain' of Captain and Tennille

Oh, I get by with a little help from my friends. Mmm I'm gonna try with a little help from my friends. Oh I get high with a little help from my friends.
John Lennon and Paul McCartney

These youngsters have nothing to fear if they bring drugs along to us. All we are concerned about is preventing them from getting involved with drug-taking.
Inspector George Cutliffe, Police Liaison Chief at Isle of Wight Festival, 1970

If you were on a plane and the pilot was drunk, you could tell. But if he was on marijuana, you couldn't.
Ronald Reagan

Marijuana took rock 'n' roll into the future and rock 'n' roll took marijuana to the masses so they could climb into the future and nobody's been the same since.
John Sinclair, White Panther Party

The whole hippie scene is wishful thinking. They wish they could love, but they're full of shit.
Frank Zappa

It sometimes breaks my heart that we're all singing songs about love and peace and togetherness and really there is so little of it.
Robert Plant

What we're doing is displaying a basic rock 'n' roll concept combined with lots of LSD and watching Star Trek.
The Pink Fairies

When you're listening late at night you may think the band are not quite right. But they are, they just play it like that.
John Lennon and Paul McCartney

One pill makes you larger, and one pill makes you small. And the ones that mother gives you, don't do anything at all.
Grace Slick

Electrical banana is gonna be a sudden craze
Donovan Leitch

Now she's the one who gives us all those magical things, and reads us stories out of the I Ching.
Joe MacDonald

Lucy In The Sky With Diamonds.
Song Title by John Lennon and Paul McCartney

Pot is a beautiful event. You feel it waft through a concert hall and you know someone is happy.
Pete Townshend

Actually you gotta toke down to get down, and in order to toke down you gotta get down and if you get down, we all get down.
Wayne Kramer, MC5

JOE MACDONALD/PHOTO BY DOUG MCKENZIE

DONOVAN LEITCH/PHOTO BY ROBERT ELLIS

I tried marijuana one time, but it didn't give me anything but a headache.
Glen Campbell

Coming into Los Angeles, bringing in a couple of keys. Don't touch my bags if you please, Mr. Customs Man.
Arlo Guthrie

Now if you're tired or a little run down, can't seem to get ya feet off the ground. Maybe you ought to try a little bit of LSD.
Joe MacDonald

There was so much dope and acid around in those days that I don't think anyone can remember anything about anything.
Roger Waters, Pink Floyd

We are magic. It's magic that we're walking around
Donovan

I was just a young chick. I just wanted to get it on. I wanted to smoke dope, take dope, lick dope, suck dope, fuck dope, anything I could lay my hands on I wanted to do it, man.
Janis Joplin

I see a red door and I want it painted black. No colours any more, I want them to turn black.
Mick Jagger and Keith Richard

We were passing round a joint — a doobie — and someone said 'We're all doobie brothers'. We were called Pud before that.
The Doobie Brothers

In the Top Forty half the songs are *secret* messages to the teen world to drop out, turn on and groove with the chemicals and light shows at discotheques.
Art Linkletter

Feed your head.
Grace Slick

LSD is a medicine — a different kind of medicine. It makes you aware of the universe, so to speak. You realise how foolish objects are. But LSD is not for the groovy people, it's for mad, hateful people who want revenge. It's for people who have heart attacks. They ought to use it at the Geneva Convention.
Bob Dylan

I am the eggman, oh they are the eggmen, I am the walrus. Goo, goo, g'joob.
John Lennon and Paul McCartney

Here's another clue for you all. The Walrus was Paul.
John Lennon and Paul McCartney

MICK JAGGER & KEITH RICHARD/PHOTO BY GERED MANKOWITZ

FOR A FEW DOLLARS MORE

Nobody believes me that I came into music just because I wanted the bread
Mick Jagger

Money means mostly a convenience for me. Cabs. I like getting out of a movie, if the movie is boring in the middle and not feeling I've wasted the money I've spent.
Art Garfunkel

If you've got a mind-shattering talent, you want a million dollars for it.
Elton John

I'm positive I could live very happily on £30 a week.
Cliff Richard

I hope this record sells — I'm definitely tired of sliding through life on my good looks.
Elvin Bishop

Zsa Zsa's got her jewels, Minnie's got her chickens to go. I've got my corporations, I'm a capitalist so and so.
Joni Mitchell

I'm not ashamed of being rich. I'm very materialistic. I'll tell you. I'm extremely materialistic.
Rod Stewart

They're always saying I'm a capitalistic pig. I suppose I am. But . . . it's good for my drumming.
Keith Moon

Playing the road is just like robbing Wells Fargo. You ride in, take the money and ride out.
Marty Robbins

My goal was riches in the uppermost strata.
Harry Nilsson

HARRY NILSSON/PHOTO BY DAVID GAHR

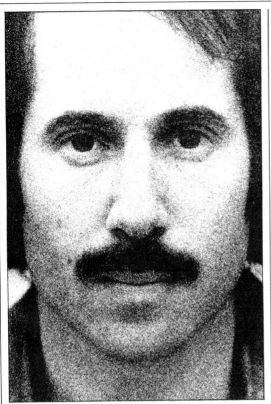

PAUL SIMON

CHARLIE WATTS

If a song lives for a couple of years, it's a pretty good thing.
Paul Simon

Who needs money when you're funny?
Randy Newman

I think Alice Cooper Cosmetics would be real neat and classy. Just think — I could appear on TV in a bath, look into the camera and advertise Alice Cooper Turtle Oil.
Alice Cooper

I have one basic drive on my side that they can't defeat — greed.
Frank Zappa

Hit records are very near and dear to me.
Pete Townshend

I don't want to be a star, I want to be a millionaire.
Richard B. 'Kinky' Friedman

So you think my singing's out of time? Well, it makes me money.
Neville Holder and James Lea

I have American ideas — I love money. The idea all along was to make one million dollars.
Alice Cooper

Money is very useful stuff to have. Actually the more you earn the less you seem to handle.
Charlie Watts

Rock and roll owes me a living.
Ron 'Pigpen' McKernan

They're paying me $50,000 a year to be like me.
Janis Joplin

I believe music is just like buying and selling groceries. Or insurance, or anything else. The better product you've got, the better people like it and the better you can sell it.
Charlie Pride

One of our aims is to stay amateurs — as soon as we become professional we'll be ruined.
Ray Davies, 1965

We would rather be rich than famous. That is, more rich and slightly less famous.
John Lennon

If you want something for nothing, go jerk off.
Bob Weir, Grateful Dead

FOR A FEW DOLLARS MORE

Our attitude to freak-outs is that we would not play at one again unless they paid us three times our normal fee.
The Pink Floyd

I have no use for bodyguards, but I have very specific use for two highly trained certified public accountants.
Elvis Presley

The only difference between 'boring' and 'laid back' is one million dollars.
Glenn Frey, Eagles

I'm so tight I don't spend a penny. I don't mind buying a round, but I can't stand buying two.
Rod Stewart

Henry Ford knows how to sell cars by advertising. I'm selling peace and Yoko and I are just one big advertising campaign. Really we're Mr. and Mrs. Peace.
John Lennon

I'm against those who were born with golden spoons in their mouths . . . they want a kick up the backside. I've earned everything myself. I've worked hard for it and I'm going to enjoy it in the next five to ten years.
Rod Stewart

On the strength of my earnings I bought an eight room house for my folks . . . I also bought an elegant grey and black Thunderbird, dental capping for two front teeth, an abstract painting by a distinguished artist, a gold wristwatch for my manager Sal Bonfede, a load of presents for my old pals in the Bronx, three tuxedos, ten pairs of slacks, seven pairs of custom-made Italian shoes with elastic on the sides and ten thousand dollars worth of expert advice to help me work up a nightclub act which I could step into adult show places.
Dion DeMucci of Dion and the Belmonts

I can make it longer if you like the style, I can change it round, and I want to be a paperback writer.
John Lennon and Paul McCartney

Like I've said before, the Moody's are a communist band run by a capitalist board.
Ray Thomas, Moody Blues

Money was a much saner goal than adoration. They'll both drive you crazy, but if I'm going to blow my brains out for five years, I want something to show for it.
Don Henley, Eagles

Just point me at the piano and give me my money and in fifteen minutes I'll have 'em shaking, shouting, shivering and shacking.
Jerry Lee Lewis

RAY THOMAS

FOR A FEW DOLLARS MORE

I better start worrying when they don't bother me any more.
Elvis Presley

My world is very small. Money can't really improve it any. Money can just keep it from being smothered.
Bob Dylan

Listen, if they're going to buy lunch-boxes, they may as well buy David Cassidy lunch-boxes.
David Cassidy

I was 62 the day they had the premiere of 'Hard Day's Night' and we all went to the Dorchester. Then Paul handed me a big parcel and I opened it and it was a picture of a horse. So I said 'Very nice' but I thought what do I want with a picture of a horse? Then Paul must have seen my face because he said 'It's not just a picture, dad, I've bought you the bloody horse.'
James McCartney

I watch my kruger-rands going up and down on the international market and I study gold prices, though it's not such a good time to buy right now . . .
Carl Palmer, Emerson Lake and Palmer, 1977

If we're selling something, it's good. We're selling escapism. Relief from nine till five problems . . . people take Valium, people buy records . . . we reach the masses, we have fun and that is valid. I sleep very soundly.
Paul Stanley, Kiss

Six million, a hundred million, it's all an illusion. It doesn't mean that much to me, really. I mean, who else is there to go and see.
Bob Dylan, on the ticket applications for his 1974 tour — 6 million for only 660,000 seats

We broke Lawrence Welk's attendance record in Abilene, Texas, and I'm very proud of that.
Gene Simmons, Kiss

About all I'll end up with is a white suit and a thousand dollars.
Mick Jagger on the Stones 1975 Tour of America, for which he actually earned around $450,000

What's money? A man is a success if he gets up in the morning and gets to bed at night and in between he does what he wants to.
Bob Dylan

BOB DYLAN

YOU, THE PEOPLE

When I look at an audience, all I see are beautiful people.
Stevie Wonder

If they don't get the words, they'll get the music, because that's really where it's at.
Brian Wilson

It's every kid's dream to have the biggest erector set.
Bill Spooner, The Tubes

If you get a clever audience, they can make you collapse.
Alvin Lee

They must love us really.
Ray Davies

It makes no difference how good you are. If you're not exposed to the public enough, then you're dead.
Johnny Shines

I've been asked if this is the last tour since I was 19 years old.
Mick Jagger

People who have memorised your songs — how can you not love them.
Todd Rundgren

We just think the mass audience has better taste than most stations do.
Tom Donahue, founder of KSAN-FM Radio, San Francisco

Somebody in that audience out there knows what we're doing, and that person is getting off on it beyond his/her wildest dreams.
Frank Zappa

When they see me they're getting five things no other act can offer.
Alice Cooper

STEVIE WONDER

YOU, THE PEOPLE

At my concerts most of the chicks are looking for liberation, they think I'm gonna show them how to do it.
Janis Joplin

I find it a bit of a drag that certain people need to project their death wishes on me. I've no preoccupation with death whatsoever.
Keith Richard

You (one side of the audience) are Life. You (the other side) are Death. I straddle the fence and my balls hurt.
Jim Morrison

Audiences are very much like the kids in Tommy's Holiday Camp — they want something without working for it.
Pete Townshend

People say we were 'magic'. I don't know, I was too busy doing it.
Roger McGuinn

An English audience is like a good fuck. You hold hands with it for a while, you kiss it, you pet it and then it pays you off.
Glenn Frey, Eagles

For all the control you have over an audience, it doesn't mean you can control the murders . . . you can't make someone's knife disappear just by looking at him, you can't be God, you can't ever pretend to play at being God.
Keith Richard

No rock musician has ever paid to see an audience, why should an audience pay to see a rock musician?
David Peel

I used to lose half my audience, right at the start, when I come screaming out of my coffin. They used to run screaming down the aisles and half kill themselves scrambling out of the exits, I couldn't stop them. In the end I had to hire some boys to sit up in the gallery with a supply of shrivelled up elastic bands and when the audience started running, my boys would drop the elastic bands onto their heads and whisper 'Worms'.
Screamin' Jay Hawkins

One time you let people know how much sense you got, right away they quit having anything to do with you.
Howlin' Wolf (Chester Burnett)

If you feel like singing along, don't.
James Taylor

You don't shoulder any responsibilities when you pick up a guitar or sing a song, because it's not a position of responsibility.
Keith Richard

The performer is strictly a product of the public's imagination. We're just a reflection of what people want. It's the audience that are fags if anything.
David Bowie

I can't seem to remember anything any more, especially this week, so let's just forget about the lyrics.
Joe Cocker at his 'Comeback' show, 1972

The most trouble is most people expect me to roam around carrying an axe. If I was Alice every time I went into a bar, turning over the tables and scaring people, I'd probably be dead by now.
Alice Cooper

If I could stick my knife in my heart, suicide right on stage, would it be enough for your teenage lust, would it help to ease the pain?
Mick Jagger and Keith Richard

You can't take a fucking record like other people take a bible.
Keith Richard

Criticism and critics, they're full of shit. If they weren't they'd be out playin' and they wouldn't have time to criticise anybody.
Felix Pappalardi

Either those cats cool it, or we don't play.
Keith Richard at Altamont

It's all music, no more, no less. I know in my own mind what I'm doing. If anyone has imagination, he'll know what I'm doing. If they can't understand my songs they're missing something. If they can't understand green clocks, wet chairs, purple lamps or hostile statues, they're missing something too.
Bob Dylan

I just have thoughts in my head and I write them. I'm not trying to lead any causes for anyone else.
Bob Dylan

LOU REED

Half of these people turn up at concerts to see if I'm going to drop dead on stage and they're so disappointed that I'm still around and writing and capable of performing without falling down and stumbling around. But I haven't OD'd . . . Those people, they wanted me to OD, and they never offered me the dope to do it with.
Lou Reed

The way it was going for a while I thought I might end up appearing on stage in spangles and beads. I'd rather wear a sportscoat.
Lou Reed

To me our music is like Jamaican stuff — if they can't hear it, they're not supposed to hear it. It's not for them if they can't understand it.
Joe Strummer, The Clash

I don't feel I have any responsibility, no. Whoever it is that listens to my songs owes *me* nothing . . . I've never written any song that begins with the words 'I've gathered you here tonight'.
Bob Dylan

I know I'm never gonna be able to beat them. I don't believe in other people. They are morons. They must be to stand for all this.
Joe Strummer, The Clash

You can't go beyond your limitations. They want me to try an artistic picture. That's fine, maybe I can pull it off one day. But not now. I've done eleven pictures and they've all made money. A certain type of audience likes me. I entertain them with what I'm doing. I'd be a fool to tamper with that kind of success.
Elvis Presley 1963

I thought everybody had heard them.
Bob Dylan on 1975 release of heavily bootlegged 'Basement Tapes'

What we all fail to understand is that the majority of rock and roll stars are diaper people, relative to how to handle an audience.
Bill Graham, promoter

BOB DYLAN

As long as the people don't get bored, I don't get bored. I do my best to satisfy the people and that's what counts. They must like it or I wouldn't still be around.
Fats Domino

All we are doing is telling people to question what they are doing and if it doesn't satisfy them, to do what they want. I hate preaching, it's just encouragement.
Mick Jones, The Clash

One luxury of being a successful band is you can experiment in public sometimes.
Ray Davies

The real thing is not something that you'd want to idolize.
Lou Reed

I got my self-respect in this group. I don't believe in guitar heroes. If I walk to the front of the stage, it's because I want to reach the audience, I want to *communicate* with them. I don't want them to suck my guitar off.
Mick Jones, The Clash

We try to keep a sharp image because the public wants it. Who would have wanted to see Clark Gable without his false teeth?
Paul Stanley, Kiss

BILL GRAHAM

WHITE LINE FEVER

I'm not on drugs — I just have a nervous disorder.
Bob Dylan

I only get ill when I give up drugs.
Keith Richard

I'm not a junkie and I won't even try it out.
Neil Young

I keep wondering what the inside of my lungs looks like.
Cat Stevens, 1967

The Nixons are nice people. And they serve some good liquor.
Doug Kershaw

I've seen the bottom of a lot of bottles.
Carl Perkins

That jaded, faded junkie nurse, what pleasant company.
Mick Jagger and Keith Richard

Music is like heroin in a way. You get a taste of it and you can't hardly get away from it. And you always have that craving.
Roy Buchanan

I started attending Emory University in Atlanta — I majored at Emory in Beer, with a minor in Rock 'n' Roll.
Mac Davis

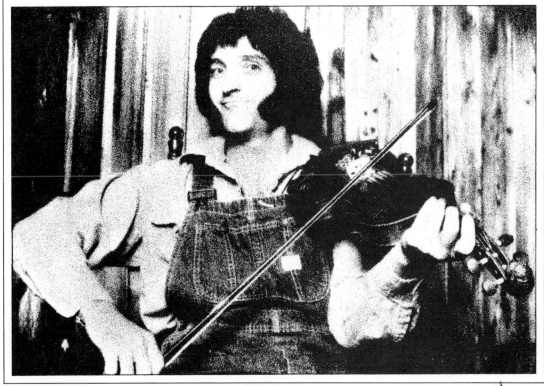

DOUG KERSHAW

JOHNNY CASH

At first I'd take those pills so I wouldn't be shy when I went on stage. They seemed to give me guts or I thought they did, but it was all a false feeling. Each pill you take burns up a bit of a man.
Johnny Cash

Well, ask me why I'm drunk all the time, it levels my head and eases my mind.
Bob Dylan

Knowing me, I'll probably get busted at my own funeral.
Jimi Hendrix

I never get drunk. Two drinks and I get a headache and fall asleep.
Lou Reed

Speed will turn you into your parents.
Frank Zappa

I think I think too much. That's why I drink.
Janis Joplin

Whatever Gets You Through The Night
John Lennon

When I first started, pills made me feel good. Every time I took them I felt good. Then I took so many that I didn't feel good. I was only awake.
Johnny Cash

I started out on burgundy, but soon hit the harder stuff.
Bob Dylan

Blessed are the meth drinkers, pot sellers, illusion dwellers. O Lord, why have you forsaken me?
Paul Simon

I'm a trainee alcoholic.
Al Stewart

I'll be in a basement room with a needle and a spoon, and another girl can take my pain away.
Mick Jagger and Keith Richard

I'm fixing a hole where the rain comes in and stops my mind from wandering where it will go.
John Lennon and Paul McCartney

God help the troubador who tries to be a star.
Phil Ochs

I like whiskey and I like the gin, but I don't much care for the state I'm in.
Dave Swarbrick and B. Rowland

I takes whiskey for my breakfast and whiskey's good for you if you drink it right. Four drinks a day, it keeps you feeling good.
Robert Pete Williams.

I only gave up drugs when the doctor told me I had six months to live.
Keith Richard

People think I lead a dissipated life. That's not true. Drugs are a cheat. I can see it right away in the colour of the skin, in the quality of the hair, the nails, the brilliance of the eyes. Look at me — do I look like a heroin addict?
Bianca Jagger

I love my country stuff. I just sing my pretty love songs and my drinking songs and leave it at that.
Jerry Lee Lewis

Although I'm so tired I'll have another cigarette and curse Sir Walter Raleigh, he was such a stupid get.
John Lennon and Paul McCartney

Just give me one more sniffie, another sniffie of that dope. I'll catch a cow like a cowboy, throw a bull without a rope.
Victoria Spivey

Coke's good for horses, not for women or men. The doctor said it'll kill you, but he didn't say when.
Anonymous, 1930's

When you need a little coke and sympathy.
Mick Jagger and Keith Richard

Everybody's got something to hide except for me and my monkey.
John Lennon and Paul McCartney

Led Zeppelin's success may be attributable at least in part to the accelerating popularity of barbiturates and amphetamines — drugs that render their users most responsive to crushing volume and ferocious histrionics.
Los Angeles Times

The skinhead girl made it clear that she only came here for the beer.
The Faces

The beer that made Milwaukee famous has made a loser out of me.
Jerry Lee Lewis

I don't take drugs. I've seen great musicians become nothing but snivelling, diseased mongrels because of drugs. It's only a lesser person that takes drugs and no way am I gonna be that.
Ted Nugent

She blew my nose and then she blew my mind.
Mick Jagger and Keith Richard

No more running for the shelter of your mother's little helper.
Mick Jagger and Keith Richard

Heroin. It's my life and it's my wife.
Lou Reed

In a cold dirty room. That's where I found myself, with a bottle of wine and some pills on the shelf.
Gram Parsons and Chris Hillman

If I spring a leak she mends me, I don't have to speak 'cos she defends me, a drunkard's dream if I ever did see one.
Robbie Robertson

ROBBIE ROBERTSON

Pills? I take pills all the time. I'll show you my briefcase — I'm a doctor, aspirin, anything, I take it.
Ray Davies

I think I lost some weight there and I'm sure I need some rest. Sleeping don't come easy in a straight white vest.
Alice Cooper and Michael Bruce

I got nasty habits. I take tea at three.
Mick Jagger and Keith Richard

Can't you see, Sister Morphine, I'm trying to score.
Mick Jagger and Keith Richard

Forty-nine times with ad lib shouts of 'oh', 'oo', 'no', yells, moans, shrieks, groans, etc.
Coda, sheet music for 'Cold Turkey' by John Lennon

I seen through junkies, I been through it all. I seen religion from Jesus to Paul. Don't let them fool you with dope and cocaine, can't do you no harm to feel your own pain.
John Lennon

I got silence on my radio. Let the airwaves flow.
Mick Jagger and Keith Richard

I'm not into dope. That's true . . . I don't smoke grass and I don't like the things that everyone sniffs off a table. That's tawdry. It's so *common*. I like to play with my own system. Alone, I'm into drug masturbation.
Lou Reed

Les, the police are coming in through the windows.
Mick Jagger's phone call to publicist Les Perrin during his 1968 bust

Who can you talk to on the road? Long haired drug people where ever you look. The boy passes over a bag of green powder and passes out. Don't take that, it has horse tranquiliser in it. Oh, I shot up to your song. I got busted to your song. Oh, please bless me and touch me and make it all go away. I loved to you.
Lou Reed

It was kinda like stuffing the wrong card in a computer, when you're sticking these artificial stimulants in your arm.
Dion DiMucci

RAY DAVIES

You know we were rehearsing, and we are running through 'Waiting For The Man' . . . you know 'Twenty-six dollars in my hand' . . . and I said 'Hey, wait a minute, *twenty-six dollars???*' I mean, you can't even get a *blow job* for twenty-six dollars these days, let alone some smack.
Lou Reed, 1977

I like to think of cocaine as the thinking man's Dristan.
Wavy Gravy (Hugh Romney)

You know I'd really love to hear Frank Sinatra do 'Heroin'. Really. It would be just *incredible* to hear *Frank Sinatra* coming out with that song on some middle of the road radio station. Because that song doesn't mince words.
Lou Reed

BLACKS & BLUES

Can Blue Men Sing The Whites?
Viv Stanshall, Bonzo Dog Band

Can't no white man sing the blues and can't no Negro sing no love song.
Hound Dog Taylor

I don't think you can feel the blues until you been though some hard times.
Muddy Waters

You know . . . young people thought the blues was English.
Memphis Slim

The whites just *startin'* to get the blues.
John Lee Hooker

I've never really considered myself a blues singer, I still don't, I'm a folk singer if I'm anything.
Rod Stewart

Motown kind of made Detroit a little more than a motor city. Before that all we had was cars.
Martha Reeves

The blues are almost sacred to some people, but others don't understand and when I can't make them understand it makes me feel bad because they mean so much to me.
B. B. King

Blues grabbed mamachild, tore him all upside down.
Robert Johnson

To get the bottleneck you first have to have an empty bottle. I'd get drunk and cut my fingers playing.
Jo Willie Wilkins

I don't dig down-home no more. It's so embarrassing.
One of the Four Tops

Soul ain't nothin' but a feelin'. It gets in your hand, makes you clap your hand. Gets in your feet, makes you move your feet. That's all it is.
Wilson Pickett

Rastafarians eat their babies.
Patti Labelle

I'll play it first and tell you what it is later.
Miles Davis

All my life I was having trouble with women . . . I've done a lot of writing about women. Then, after I quit having trouble with them, I could feel in my heart that someone would always have trouble with them, so I kept writing those blues.
Muddy Waters

I stick to my blues as blues and I'm not afraid to play them because I'm scared I'm gonna go to the burnin' place, whatever it is. I'm not afraid of that.
Henry Townshend

Yeah my life is like a toilet bowl. Ain't got no money, all I got is soul.
Anon

I couldn't do no yodellin' so I turned to howlin' and it's done me just fine.
Howlin' Wolf (Chester Burnett)

You can't be the best. You can just be a good 'un.
Muddy Waters

I always thought I had a gift but I wasn't sure until I made my first number, which was 'Boogie Chillun'. Then I was definitely sure . . . Gosh I was hot as a firecracker then.
John Lee Hooker

RAY CHARLES/PHOTO BY ANNIE LEIBOVITZ

Can a white man sing the blues? I don't care a damn if he's green or purple — he can give it to ya.
Ray Charles

The whites loused up a whole art form for twenty years.
John Hammond

'A good man is hard to hold' moans Ida Cox in her latest Paramount record. Hear her threats against the gals who lead him wrong. Some man! Some blues!
Paramount ad for their Race Records, 1920s

I'm still deliverin', 'cos I've got a long memory.
Muddy Waters

For a fact rock 'n' roll ain't no different from the blues. We just pepped it up a lot . . . it's all trends, they come and go. It seems that like every twenty years the world jumps off and gets happy. It's going to explode again. You just be there when it jumps.
Big Joe Turner

You see I done get too old to get a job. Now I really got to stay with the music.
Howlin' Wolf (Chester Burnett)

The blues is the truth. You'd better believe what they're telling you is the truth.
Buddy Guy

All blues singers are great liars.
Memphis Slim

If I didn't know some of the SNCC people, I would have gone on thinking that Martin Luther King was nothing more than some under-privileged war hero.
Bob Dylan

I'm the man who put the unk into the funk.
Muddy Waters

I learnt to play the guitar about 1909. I learnt myself — didn't take long to learn. I just stayed up one night and learnt myself.
Peg Leg Howell

I'm just an old fellow from the corn fields and I don't know how to play nothing fancy. Just some old blues.
Yank Rachell

Certain words have been spoken from the mouth of the member of the Houses of Parliament saying he will donate £1,000 for each black man to go home . . . any time you seh we mus go home, we are willing to go home, but we are awaiting on you to give us the Black Star liner . . .

Tapper Zukie

The songs have to tell a story. Just like 'Boom Boom'. I used to come into a bar and there was a barmaid used to come in nights, she was a very nice kid, a friend of mine. Some nights you know I would come in late. She'd say 'Oh, Boom Boom' — just like that — 'The boss gonna get you'. She kept saying that over and over and I just put one and two together.

John Lee Hooker

You don't want to be too worried, and you don't want to be too satisfied either, but you want to have your mind a little mixed up just enough to keep from being too bothered or too happy.

Bukka White

That's where the blues start: it don't start in no city, now. Don't never get that wrong. It started right behind one of them mules or one of them log houses, one of them log camps or the levee camp. That's where the blues sprung from. I know what I'm talking about.

Bukka White

This was my hobby — guitar. It was a thing I was born with. Yes, it came easy to me.

John Lee Hooker

You don't have to be in trouble a lot of time to have a worried mind. You can just get to sitting down there thinking about things . . .

Bukka White

I told more truth in my blues than the average person tells in his church songs . . . sometimes I think the average person sings a church song just for the tune, not for the words, but the blues is sung not for the tune. It's sung for the words, mostly. A real blues singer sings a blues for the words.

Reverend Rubin Lacy

I knew the time when there just wasn't any white musicians much.

Reverend Rubin Lacy

What is the blues then? It's a worried mind. It boils down to worry.

Reverend Rubin Lacy

I had a guy tell me once, he say 'A man that writes a song, he has a photograph mind'. Which I think he's just about right. I can lay down and I can see things in my mind and then from that I can write a poem. It don't even have to happen actually to me or never happen to no-one else. It's something that could happen.

Leroy Dallas

I believe it will be a long time before a good, kind-hearted natural women like her will come along. She was a hard women who really loved her work. She was a real showman. Singing, dancing, doing straight comedy, and take any part in the show. She had a sweet personality . . . she was a great audience pleaser everywhere she went.

Jack Gee remembers his wife, Bessie Smith

Most of the songs that I played and I composed is from my own self-experience and that's why I guess my music sounds a little different and plays a little different and it seems to some to sound a little complicated because it is just my own — it's no copycat.

Skip James

I made up a lot of the songs I sing. It's like you hear a record or something, well you pick out some words out of that record that you like. You sing that and add something else onto it. It's just like if you're going to pray and mean it — things will be in your mind; as fast as you can get one word out, something else will come in there. Songs should tell the truth.

Fred McDowell

Our folks was in slavery a long time ago . . . it's all they could do on the field or farm is moan. That's the only way they could express their minds and get a little happy, to sing sad songs.

John Lee Hooker

IKE & TINA TURNER/PHOTO BY MICK GOLD

The kind of soul I'm talking about has got the grease. Ain't nothin' no good without the grease.
Tina Turner

Even in my blues story I must recognize God who gave us our five senses. In our dreams, when we are asleep, he is the one who talks with all of us. So many people today think the blues come from America, but they come all the way from that unholy city of Bablem.
Curtis Jones

In my opinion blues is a thing . . . you have the blues about something. Maybe you're broke, you're disgusted, you have bills, you're losing your home, your car, your girlfriend — that's the blues . . . blues come out of sadness, trouble, misfortune . . .
John Lee Hooker

In South Carolina they hung coloured people when they felt like it; in Georgia they staked them.
Reverend Gary Davis

The average coloured kid, it feels like the blues is embarrassing to them. This is my story. I think they dig it, but they feel it's embarrassing, because their fore-parents and great grandparents were brought up in slavery. They like it but they feel that in the modern day they shouldn't listen to it. They feel it drags them back.
John Lee Hooker

You'll excuse me. I don't consider myself to be a black performer. I consider myself to be a performer who is black.
Stevie Wonder

I have never given up the idea of being good at the business.
Johnny Shines

I sit down an' make up a thousand songs — anybody ask me what I did, I don't know, so you just got to give 'em a name. Because I don't know what it is. I'll just sing and play something. Funny thing, playing music. As long as I'm playing someone else's records, I know what I'm gonna play, but when I gonna play something of my own, I don't know what it's gonna be until I start playing it.
Blind Jimmie Brewer

STEVIE WONDER

I don't know why it's happened. It's something I can't figure out myself. But as time marches by they understand the meaning of the blues . . .
John Lee Hooker

I write my own tunes. Everything I got is original. It's a funny thing, you can say a word — it wouldn't mean anything to you — I can take that one word and rhyme it right down the line, just rhyme it from word to word . . . just one word you speak.
John Lee Hooker

The way I used to get Lighnin' Slim to cut blues was this. Two or three days before I'd call him for a session, I'd give his woman $25 to give him hell. If at the session he really sang the blues, because that woman had given them to him, I'd give her another $25. If she really made a good job of it, I'd give her the prettiest dress she'd ever seen on top of that.
Jay D. Miller, producer of many Deep South blues artists.

I liked the music and my daddy used to play and I used to watch him . . . I started going to country dances and listening to musicians playing and I wanted to do it too, 'cos it looked like they had such a good time playing and drinking.
David 'Honeyboy' Edwards

When I sing the blues, when I'm singing the real blues, I'm singing what I feel. Some people maybe want to laugh, maybe I don't talk so good and they don't understand, you know? But when we sing the blues — when I sing the blues it come from the heart. From right here in your soul an' if you singing what you really feel it come out all over. It ain't just what you saying, it pours out of you. Sweat runnin' down your face.
Muddy Waters

They just copy me, and I can't learn anything from them.
Little Walter

Blues have been going on for centuries and centuries, and the blues was written years and centuries ago — they was always there.
Boogie Woogie Red

I can read a little, and write, but it hasn't held me back too much — not having much schooling. I've been able to get through life on mother wit. And I always did have the gift of music.
Johnny Young

If I sing the blues and tell the truth, what have I done? What have I committed? I haven't lied.
Henry Townsend

A man who's singin' the blues — I think it's a sin 'cause it cause other people to sin.
Lil Son Jackson

I just don't like it, jumpin' on to a spiritual after I been singin' the blues. I have to wait. Because you can't mess with the Lord and I think that's messin' him up, singing blues and spirituals both.
Robert Peter Williams

People keep asking me where the blues started and all I can say is that when I was a boy we always was singing in the fields. Not real singing, you know, just hollerin', but we made up our songs about things that was happening to us at the time, and I think that's where the blues started.
Son House

I used to be a preacher. I was brought up in a church and I started preaching before I started this junk. Well I got into a little bad company one time and they said 'Aw, c'mon, take a little nip with us'. I says 'Naw'. 'Aw, c'mon'. So I took a little nip . . . And then I began to wonder, now how can I stand up in the pulpit, and preach to them, tell them how to live, and quick as I dismiss the congregation, and I see ain't nobody looking and I'm doing the same thing . . . I can't hold God in one hand the Devil in the other one. Them two guys don't get along together too well. I got to turn one of them loose. So I got out of the pulpit.
Son House

The kind of blues I play, there's no money in it. You makes a good living when you gets established like I am, but you don't get that kind of overnight million-dollar thing, man . . . no way.
Muddy Waters

MIRROR MIRROR

I am the biggest, the baddest and the fastest in the land.
Bo Diddley

I've got fifty-six gold singles, and fourteen gold albums and if anyone out there doubts it, if you ever come through Memphis you can come in and argue about it, 'cos I've got every one of them hanging on the wall.
Elvis Presley

Real estate is the only thing that doesn't depreciate — other than me.
Jerry Lee Lewis

I'm just the same as ever — loud, electrifying and full of personal magnetism.
Little Richard

My bullshit is worth most people's diamonds.
Lou Reed

I don't have to compete with psychedelia. I have surpassed it. I have talent.
P. J. Proby (James Marcus Smith)

I don't think people mind if I'm conceited. Every rock 'n' roll star in the world is conceited.
Mick Jagger

I don't care who buys the records as long as they get to the black people so I will be remembered when I die.
Miles Davies

It's so fabulous being young and a girl and you can have nice clothes and can dress up and that's the nicest part about it, being famous and people admiring you.
Sandie Shaw

I don't need people to tell me how good I am. I've worked it out for myself.
Eric Clapton

I haven't got a smiling mouth or a talking face.
Ringo Starr

I guarantee that if Elvis had his choice of being up in heaven right now, or coming on before me, he'd have to come on before me. There's no way Elvis can follow me.
Jerry Lee Lewis

When I was a boy I was the hero in comic books and movies. I grew up believing in that dream. Now I've lived it out. That's all a man can ask for.
Elvis Presley

I can do anything. One of these days I'll be so complete I won't be human. I'll be a god.
John Denver

I'm thinking of getting a place here in the States, just to drop off my suitcase.
Peter Frampton

I am the Lizard King; I can do anything.
Jim Morrison

I am Johnny Cool, y'know.
Phil Lynott, Thin Lizzy

Me and Nureyev have flaming rows about whether it takes more talent and discipline to be a ballet dancer or a pop singer.
Mick Jagger

Ego is not a four-letter word.
Don Steele, Top 40 DJ on KHJ, Los Angeles

I was the best wiggler in the world.
Marc Bolan

MIRROR, MIRROR...

I really believe that I have more talent in my little finger than Tony Bennett or anybody like that can possibly ever hope to achieve in a lifetime.
Elton John

I'm honest, real up front. I party. I get high. I'm a street person. You understand what I mean? I preach love. When you do right, you come out right. When you love, you live.
Wolfman Jack (Robert W. Smith)

God, I don't know . . . we just play and it's swell.
Mark Farner, Grand Funk Railroad

I never felt better in my life. I still have all my hair and everything. I don't really think about it. I just feel dynamite.
Fabian Forte, on turning 30

Listen, we're a garage band, and we're proud of it.
Patti Smith

I love being a star more than life itself.
Janis Joplin

I have a lick that's better than Jeff Beck's and Jeff has a lick that's better than mine, but Jimi Hendrix is better than either of us.
Eric Clapton

I love arrogance, and I'll get it back.
Ian Hunter, Mott the Hoople

My American public isn't ready for me.
Long John Baldry

I thought we stood for infinity.
Mick Jagger

I could have been a great song-writer. I reckon I could have been one of the greatest. I still write some. I just don't record any of them. Because I prefer to concentrate on my entertaining instead.
Jerry Lee Lewis

I am today's powerful young man, I am today's successful young man.
Pete Townshend

I know I'm country — I can look at my bare feet and tell that.
Skeeter Davis

Hell, I'm only country.
Jerry Lee Lewis, responding to the press outcry after his marriage to his cousin Myra, aged 13

As long as my picture is on the front page, I don't care what they say about me on page ninety-six.
Mick Jagger

There is nothing about my career that is an accident.
Marc Bolan

We're the poets of Now. You read Yeats or what's his name and you can't make out a word.
Graham Nash

IAN HUNTER/PHOTO BY L.F.I.

GRAHAM NASH

I'm the kind of guy who'd sell you a rat's asshole for a wedding ring.
Tom Waits

If I wasn't me, I would have idolised myself in the Velvets.
Lou Reed

I think for the first three years the Fish were one of the most influential rock bands there'd ever been.
Country Joe MacDonald

Everything I know I taught myself.
Bo Diddley

There is no critic in the world that knows as much as I do.
Miles Davies

I taught myself everything about piano. I was not influenced by anyone. I lived so far back in the country, I don't think I knew anyone who could influence me.
Jerry Lee Lewis

We always thought there was more to playing rock 'n' roll than playing 'Johnny B. Goode'.
The Pink Floyd

What else you gonna do? Work in a gas station?
Frank Zappa, replying to opinions that his work schedule was very heavy for a rock musician.

Ours is the folk music of the technological age.
Jimmy Page

Please allow me to introduce myself I'm a man of wealth and taste.
Mick Jagger and Keith Richard

T. Rex is a monster, and I'm the whip-master.
Marc Bolan

It can be my gimmick, so at least I won't be overlooked. Whether I'm good or bad, you will see me coming. And you will know it when I walk in.
Dolly Parton on her massive blonde wig, her trademark

BRUCE SPRINGSTEEN

I'm not being big-headed, but the Kinks were unique . . . it's like getting to the North Pole first. Really, until we started diversifying, we couldn't be touched. We were a better group afterwards, but we became touchable.
Ray Davies

I'm told that I'm a parody of myself. But who better to parody? If I'm going to mimic somebody, I might as well mimic somebody good. Like myself. I can do Lou Reed better than most people, and a lot of people try.
Lou Reed

How did I turn into this person, man . . . Sometimes I look at my face and I think it looks pretty run down, but considering all I have been through, I don't look bad at all.
Janis Joplin

I didn't change my name in honour of Dylan Thomas, that's just a story. I've done more for Dylan Thomas than he's done for me. Look how many kids are probably reading his poetry now because they heard that story.
Bob Dylan

Sometimes I just like being Lou Reed better than I like being anyone else.
Lou Reed

We can't be roguish underdogs any more. We have to be gracious winners.
Glenn Frey, Eagles

So may I introduce to you the one and only Billy Shears.
John Lennon and Paul McCartney

I've got a car, a motorcycle, a truck, a house — what more could I possibly want?
Bruce Springsteen, 1977

I never *work*, man. I *vacation* all the time. I'm *vacationing* right now!
Wolfman Jack (Robert W. Smith)

Happy Xmas to all those starving hairdressers and their families.
Ad for Rolling Stones in 'New Musical Express', early 1960s

I epitomise America.
John Denver

I'll tell you the truth. I'm gonna do what I wanna do, no matter what anyone says.
Jerry Lee Lewis

I have a lot of respect for my own opinion.
Paul Stanley, Kiss

This is Middle America, man. They're sicker than we are.
Peter Criss, Kiss

I'm Mr. Motown. Who are you. I played on million sellers.
Michael Henderson

IT'S ONLY ROCK 'N' ROLL

Rock is so much fun . . . that's what it's all about — filling up the chest cavities and the empty kneecaps and elbows.
Jimi Hendrix

Music is all goo that you have to shape.
Captain Beefheart (Don Van Vliet)

Let's face it — rock 'n 'roll is bigger than all of us.
Alan Freed

It has no beginning and no end for it is the very pulse of life itself.
Larry Williams on Rock 'n' Roll

You can intellectualise about a lot of rock 'n' roll music but it's primarily not an intellectual thing. It's music, that's all.
Jann Wenner, editor 'Rolling Stone' magazine

I was in the studio one day at 1706 Union and my secretary noticed that young man going by, very shy, and he wanted to make this record for his mother's birthday.
Sam Phillips, head of Sun Records on the arrival of Elvis Presley

It's what's happening . . .
Catchphrase for Murray the K, 1960s DJ

I've heard incredible Rolling Stones stories I knew nothing about. I don't know if I was asleep in my room or what — why did I miss out on that one?
Keith Richard

Pop music is sex and you have to hit them in the face with it.
Andrew Loog Oldham

JIMI HENDRIX WITH NOEL REDDING & MITCH MITCHELL

It's not much of a way to see the country is it? All you care about is how good the bed is and can you get something to eat after the show.
Charlie Watts, touring America, 1972

I was worried, because we didn't have anything. Those sweet numbers didn't have that *thing*. They were great but they didn't have that thing. We went over to this place to eat — the Dewdrop Inn — and the place was empty and this cat got up to the piano and began singing 'Womp bomp a lu mop, a bomp bam boom'.
Bumps Blackwell on Little Richard's first session for Speciality Records, 1956

Ladies and gentlemen, I'd like to do a song now that tells a little story, that really makes a lot of sense . . . Awopbopaloobopalopbamboom!! Tootie Fruttie!! All Rootie!!
Little Richard on TV, 1956

Ambition: To join Little Richard.
Bob Dylan's High School Year Book, Class of '59

There's a lot of things blamed on me that never happened. But then, there's a lot of things that I did that I never got caught at.
Johnny Cash

If it's warm enough for us to move our fingers, we usually like to play.
Jack Casady, Hot Tuna

Music is a safe kind of high.
Jimi Hendrix

Music is everybody's mother.
Donovan

Anything called a 'Hootenanny' ought to be shot on sight.
'Time Magazine', 1962

I guess it's OK man, at least it has a beat.
Benny Goodman 'The King of Swing' on Rock 'n' Roll

I'll never get tired of playing this music. I'm never gonna stop playing it. I'll go on playing just as long as there are people to listen.
Jerry Lee Lewis

Country music is Americana. It's Hollywood and Tin Pan Alley and hillbilly blended together in the diamond that is country music. I believe our fans are made out of a little better timber than others. The barn stands longer.
Merle Travis

We play rock and roll. We don't go any deeper than that.
John Fogerty, Creedence Clearwater Revival

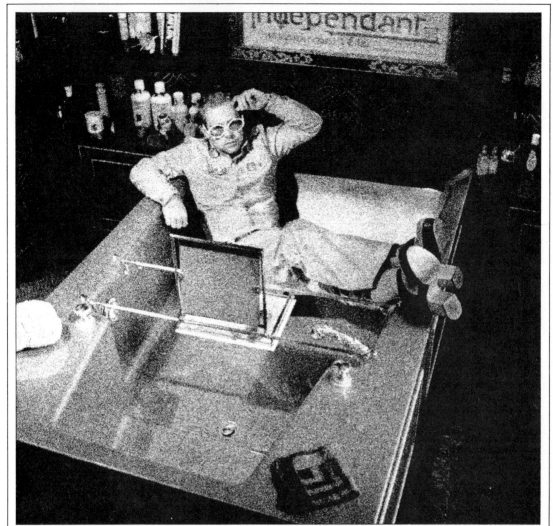

ELTON JOHN/PHOTO BY PHIL FRANKS

I've always said that pop music is disposable and it is, and that's the fun of pop music. If it wasn't disposable, it'd be a pain in the fuckin' ass.
Elton John

I don't see that rock 'n' roll should be a bad influence on anyone. It's just entertainment and the kids who like to identify their youthful high spirits with a solid beat are thus possibly avoiding other pursuits which could be harmful to them.
Bill Haley, 1959

I like ballads and I know people that like them too. I'm hip to the fact that people like a love song.
Paul McCartney

Ours is a group with built-in hate.
The Who, 1965

Well it's one for the money, two for the show, three to get ready, now go cat go!
Carl Perkins

Don't interpret me. My songs don't have any meaning. They're just words.
Bob Dylan

The rowdy element was represented by 'Rock Around The Clock', theme song of the controversial film 'Blackboard Jungle'. The rock 'n' roll school in general concentrated on a minimum of melodic line and the maximum of rhythmic noise, deliberately competing with the artistic ideals of the jungle itself.
'Encyclopaedia Brittanica' Review of 1956

I think rock 'n' roll is all frivolity — it *should* be about pink satin suits and white socks.
Mick Jagger

I don't think any musician plays anything that is new. Everything musical has been played.
Dr. John (Mac Rebannack)

They're just songs. Songs that are transparent so you can see every bit through them.
Bob Dylan

Awright, wrap up this turkey before I puke.
Bob Ezrin, producing Lou Reed's 'Berlin' album

If you want to become a piano player, go out and buy a Cecil Taylor record.
Frank Zappa

So tell me about these punk rock bands. Is the *music* any good?
Bette Midler

The slow, sad song about 'That Boy' which figures prominently in Beatle programmes is expressively unusual for its lugubrious music, but harmonically it is one of their most intriguing, with its chains of pandiatonic clusters, and the sentiment is acceptable because it is voiced cleanly and crisply.
William Mann, London 'Times' music critic

Punk rock? Oh, I've been in it for years, dear . . . Actually I saw the Sex Pistols at the 100 Club and I thought they were pretty good. Well, not *good,* but y'know, they could be.
Mick Jagger

Rock 'n' roll certainly isn't going to change the world by itself. It's not even that interested in trying.
Todd Rundgren

Messages become a drag, like preaching. I think one of the worst possible beliefs is that pop stars know any more about life than anyone else. The thing to do is to move people, to really turn them on, to subject them to a fantastic experience, to stretch their imagination.
Nick Mason, Pink Floyd

We want to be known as the pop group that launched the 1970s.
Jimmy Page, Led Zeppelin

Mild barbarians is how we were once described, and I can't really deny it.
Jimmy Page

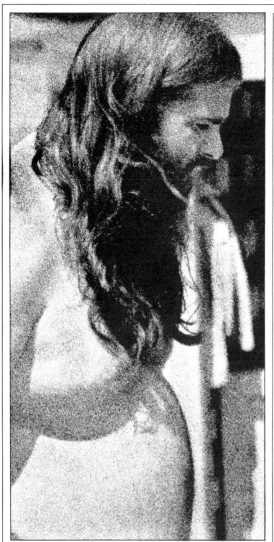

BOB HITE

They wanted me to take a picture with Mama Cass nude, that's one I refused. But I have done more outrageous things in this band than anybody else in rock 'n' roll.
Bob 'The Bear' Hite, Canned Heat

You know, the rock revolution did happen, it really did. Trouble was, nobody realised.
David Bowie

The whole idea of poetry just makes me gag.
Frank Zappa

You say that music's for the birds, you can't understand the words. Well honey, if you did, you'd really blow your lid. Baby that is rock 'n' roll.
Leiber and Stoller

Sometimes I jump on the guitar. Sometimes I grind the strings up against the frets. The more it grinds, the more it whines. Sometimes I rub myself up against the amplifier. Sometimes I play the guitar with my teeth or with my elbow. I can't remember all the things I do.
Jimi Hendrix

If you can't say it in a three-minute song, you can't say it at all.
Noddy Holder, Slade

Anyone who says rock 'n' roll is a passing fad or a flash in the pan trend along the music roads has rocks in the head, dad.
Alan Freed

Well it's Saturday night and I just got paid, fool about my money don't try to save.
Robert Blackwell and John Marascalco

It's hard getting a musician to play ugly. It contradicts all his training.
Frank Zappa

My ancestors painted themselves blue. You just get up off your arse and wail.
John Martyn

Rock 'n' roll is an asylum for emotional imbeciles.
Richard Neville, later editor 'OZ Magazine'

That record sounds like God hit the world and the world hit God back.
Phil Spector on 'River Deep Mountain High'

Rock and roll music is about rebellion. Years ago it was listening to Elvis Presley when we were supposed to be listening to Pat Boone.
John Sinclair, manager MC5

It can be explained in just one word 'sincerity'. When a hillbilly sings a crazy song, he feels crazy. When he sings 'I Laid My Mother Away' he sees her a-laying right there in the coffin . . . you got to know a lot about hard work. You got to have smelt a lot of mule manure before you can sing like a hillbilly.
Hank Williams

As far as I'm concerned with the punks, their audiences either leave immediately or are simply amused by the level of rock comedy . . . parody, you name it.
Tom Verlaine, Television

DEBBIE HARRY

If you can really get it together in three minutes . . . that's what pop songs are all about.
Debbie Harry, Blondie

There are more clowns than good guys in music. British bands don't play as well as American bands. Rock 'n' roll is simply an attitude — you don't have to play the greatest guitar.
Johnny Thunder, Heartbreakers

For the reality of what is happening today in America, we must go to rock 'n' roll, to popular music.
Ralph J. Gleason

I have to do everything in three years. After three years you just have to assume it's going to go down.
Elton John, 1971

Back to Mono.
Phil Spector

Like I didn't write 'School Days' in a classroom. I wrote it in the Street Hotel, one of the big, black low-priced hotels in St. Louis.
Chuck Berry

Rock 'n' roll is the music that inspired me to play music. There is nothing conceptually better than rock 'n' roll. No group, be it the Beatles, Dylan or the Stones have ever improved on 'Whole Lotta Shakin'' for my money. Or maybe, like our parents, that's my period and I'll dig it and never leave it.
John Lennon

We ain't looking for swastikas, just rock 'n' roll. Before 1955 it was only authors that made important statements.
Mick Jones, The Clash

The New York Dolls proved you don't need to be technically far ahead of anyone else to be accepted. We know our five chords.
Johnny Thunder, The Heartbreakers

I remember the first time I saw the Stones. Our leader said 'Don't watch them — they're a skiffle group'.
Ray Davies

Teddy Boys convinced us we didn't want nothing to do with classical rock and roll, it was so mindless . . . they thought if you didn't wear a drape suit it wasn't classical rock 'n' roll, but no singers ever dressed like that. Chuck Berry never wore a drape suit.
Wilko Johnson, Dr. Feelgood

It ain't punk, it ain't New Wave. It's the next step and the logical progression for groups to move in. Call it what you want — all the terms stink. Just call it rock 'n' roll.
Mick Jones, The Clash

It's better than fighting.
Wilko Johnson, Dr. Feelgood

The music is all. People should die for it. People are dying for everything else, so why not the music?
Lou Reed

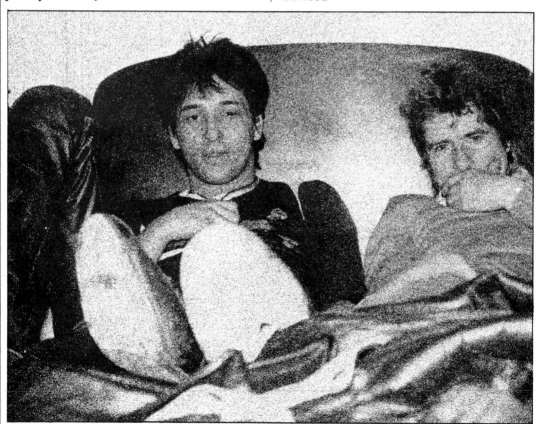

JOHNNY THUNDER

PRINTED IN ENGLAND BY:
LOWE & BRYDONE (PRINTERS) LIMITED, THETFORD, NORFOLK